CREATING ENCORES

CREATING ENCORES

A WAKE UP CALL FOR WOMEN LEADERS

Sally Arnold

Published by Creating Encores

First published 2013
This edition published 2014

© Sally Arnold

The moral right of the author has been asserted.

A Cataloguing-in-Publication record is available from the
National Library of Australia.

ISBN: 978 1 925 02790 7 (pbk)
      978 1 925 02791 4 (ebk–ePub)
      978 1 925 02792 1 (ebk–mobi)

Edited by Lisa Cropman

Cover designed by Veseliu Irina Maria

Typeset and printed by Palmer Higgs
palmerhiggs.com.au

Distributed by Dennis Jones and Associates
dennisjones.com.au

To all the women of the world who
have stood up and faced challenges head on,
both professional and personal, then had
the courage to follow their inner passion
and purpose in living a more creative,
inspired lifestyle.

Dear Daniel,
Enjoy the read!
Sally x.

Contents

Introduction

Forty seems to be the magical age when we are suddenly faced with the questions, *'What will I do for the rest of my life? Do I stay in the same career and relationship? Do I want to live in the same city, town or part of the world?*

This state of questioning – or realisation – is called a 'Wake Up Call'.

In our 20s and 30s we move along in our career and personal life with a focus on developing and using our business skills. Life is progressing well. However, as we approach our 40s, we realise that life is not as fulfilling as it could be.

In your case, maybe you've stayed safe by working in a predictable environment or career that initially excited and interested you; or perhaps you've spent time bringing up a family. Now you feel that the ladder is against the wrong wall, how do you find support and a way forward? How do you move past these crossroads in your life?

Ask yourselves these questions: *'Am I treading water? Do I want to look back on my life in 10 years and find that I'm stuck in the same unfulfilling career or relationship? Have I been in this space for a number of years? Have I* finally admitted that I am in a career that does not make my heart sing?' These are the questions that prompt many of us to decide to change our life.

Often this change in life is forced upon us – things are going well until, out of the blue, comes a challenge that shakes up our 'perfect world'. I know this from personal experience. As a high achieving woman I was moving ahead rapidly in my career and personal life when one day a bomb dropped. It was the year that I turned 40. My husband went into a large property development project that failed, and when this happened our whole world went pear-shaped.

Our so-called 'perfect life' was halted. I was forced to find a new path to walk along. I told the psychiatrist who was helping me move through this stage of my life, '*I don't want to walk along another path – I am happy on the one I'm on.*' Yet if this major disruption hadn't occurred, I wouldn't have been able to write this book!

I realise now that I was forced to look deeply within myself and admit that although I had achieved much, underneath I was a psychological mess. I was able to mask my feelings behind the facade of a well-presented businesswoman, particularly the great number of insecurities I had around self-belief and self-worth. They were hidden behind an enviable job, a happy marriage, designer clothes, a global lifestyle and, for many years, financial stability.

When unexpected obstacles appear in life we have a couple of options: we can pretend they're not there and just keep going, warts and all. (This is when some of us resort to self-medication – numbing the pain in a variety of ways; trying to ignore what has happened through excessive exercise, alcohol, eating, sex, shopping and more.) Or we can be courageous and acknowledge that deep within ourselves we have to do something about the state of affairs.

And when we take the plunge to move our life along, this is when the magic happens ...

It's a path that's unpredictable and full of new insights about life. And, if you are true to yourself, this is where you can really change.

I enjoy working with women who are moving along this path. Whether it means staying in their career and tweaking some of the challenges, or deciding to move out of their jobs and leveraging their skills into another career. The important thing is to make the move and not live a life that's unfulfilled, or stay in a career that's uninspiring.

This is where the importance of valuing *Creating Encores* manifests. This is the time and place to bring out the real woman within. There is no hiding when you put your hand up to change – she is there inside of you. She has all the inner creative wisdom you need. All you need to do is get to know her, and have a guide to work alongside you on this journey.

Begin to ask yourself, '*Who is she? Where has she been in my life?*' And for those of you who have a stable business and personal life, ask yourself, '*Why have I picked up this book? Do I want to find a way to tap into my inner wisdom?*

Do I need some additional resources in some areas of my life?'

When we learn how to mine the creative inspiration inside, we unearth 'grounded magic' and this is the heart of *Creating Encores*. The way forward is to follow the high-level performance techniques founded in the performing arts (a passionate mindset with discipline and focus); and combine them with a Visioning Program and insights from the Work Life Balance Wheel. Let these techniques become your toolbox for creative invigoration in all areas of your life.

In reading this book it's important to follow the four steps of the visioning program sequentially, since each builds upon the other. I suggest that as you read this book, you take time to move through each chapter, stop and stay with the learnings, and then move on as feels right for you.

This proven action plan has worked for hundreds of my coaching clients: women in high-level careers who are internationally known in the business and performing arts world. We work together on moving out of stuck places; helping to grow business; leveraging skills into new-look careers and, most importantly, finding the passionate connection to these areas of their life.

You can compare this personal and professional transformation to cooking a traditional dish using newfound herbs and spices. My cooking style was totally transformed when I discovered the Middle Eastern flavours of a former engineer turned cook, Yotam

Ottolenghi. I followed his recipes, and then experimented on my own by adding his exotic flavourings for a fantastic spin – to my existing repertoire of dishes – creating new, mouth-watering taste sensations!

The same metaphor is true for you, whatever your background and skills. By reading this book and following the exercises in each chapter, you have the potential to reinvigorate all areas of your personal and professional life. There has never been a better time than now to combine business and creative thinking to inspire women to *Create Encores.*

Go well.

About Me

When writing this book, I became aware that this section was going to be the hardest. It brings up areas of my life where I have been challenged, where I may have appeared confident and successful, yet underneath was fearful and afraid that I would stuff-up and be unable to financially support myself.

What I realised was that, if we are to lead an authentic life, tough stuff is going to happen. So how do we move through it, especially in the business world and at the age of around 40? If we have lost passion and purpose for our career, how do we find these important parts of us again? Perhaps the ladder has been against the wrong wall – a wall that has no real connection with the person we have grown to be.

I believe that we have an opportunity to get to know the woman that we truly are, warts and all; to take hold of her and steer her through challenges, knowing that there can be meaningful transformations in her life when we commit to change.

To better explain this I want to share my life story so far. It will show you how a creative and inspired high-achiever navigated a life both uplifting and challenging.

My life story script
Discovery of music and teenage years

At 10 years old I was fortunate to find a passion and purpose in music. I remember one Christmas holiday in the New Zealand seaside town of Timaru when my father took me to a music store to buy a recorder. (I like stylish things in my life, so I'm proud to recall that I chose a lovely wooden instrument and not a cheap plastic one.) I have very few childhood memories, but can still remember taking it back to the holiday house, sitting on my bed, and teaching myself to read music and play the recorder. It was one of the most exciting times of my life.

My world had changed from black and white to colour. I was in love with music and I was transformed as music took over my life. A year later, I started playing the flute and realised that I wanted to become a professional flautist.

The years that followed revolved around music and I used it to spirit me away from the realities of my life. Christchurch in the 60s was small and provincial, (I recall a visit from the New Zealand Symphony Orchestra was like a circus coming to town), and the traditional Anglican girls' school I attended encouraged us to pursue teaching, nursing or secretarial careers.

However, at 17 I met a guitarist called Jim. He and I, along with his friends, would spend hours playing jazz numbers like Dave Brubeck's *Take 5*. I dreamt of escaping to a culturally vibrant part of the world and moved to Adelaide University, moving on again not long after. I had already begun to set myself up for a life of change, reinvention and leverage of careers.

Life as a musician

I landed a job in the band of the stage show *Jesus Christ Superstar* in Sydney and transformed myself from a classically-trained musician into a rock star. I thrived in this world – and was also paid for doing something I loved which, for a young musician, was the ultimate. As well as being part of this most exciting show, I taught flute, worked as a backing musician and starred in a movie about the life of the conductor Bernard Heinze. Life was full. Men were all around and I was living the kind of life that most 22-year-olds could only dream about.

After a year in the show I moved to London to study flute and experience more exciting times. (It was then I realised that Europe was one of the joys of my life.) Once again I was exposed to a world of high-end performing arts – this time in 70s London. I studied, waitressed, and worked as an *au pair* for the television actor Warren Mitchell and his wife Connie. They were wonderful people to live with. I had only to take the children to school and help with cooking, which was fantastic as great food was one of my passions. I learnt to cook really well (especially Boeuf Bourguignon and Lemon Syllabub). I thrived there, in that house in the quaint and exclusive village of Highgate with its tennis court and swimming pool. How fortunate was I when many of my friends from New Zealand and Australia were living in basic accommodation in very ordinary parts of London?

After a year of study I came back to Sydney to work in the Elizabethan orchestra at the Opera House. Soon after, I moved to Melbourne where I performed with their sister orchestra. However, at this stage I knew that my time as a professional flautist was limited: sadly I was having hearing problems that were getting worse. I knew that I had to leave the orchestra or else get kicked out. It was a decision that, at the age of 26 made me feel alone, depressed and at a loss at what to do. I had to think of something other than music that I was passionate about.

A passion for food brings another career

Finally, I hit on my love of food and cooking. Before I left the orchestra I put together my next move: I would open a gourmet cookware shop – a shop that sold beautiful European speciality cookware. I researched the cookware market in Melbourne and though at times I knew I was out of my depth, I was determined to stick to my plan. I did – and *Sally's Cookshop* was born! It was a great little shop in South Yarra, piled high with pots, pans, white plates, glassware, and utensils hanging from the ceiling. It had the ambience of a small European-style emporium that had been around for years.

Since I had no back-up plan, I was scared and apprehensive when I opened the shop. If it failed I'd have to go back to Christchurch, something I did not want to happen. Fortunately the shop thrived and after several successful years, I was asked to join the buying team of a tired department store, *Buckley and Nunn*. My brief was to inject boutique style into the homewares division. I loved setting up a bigger version of *Sally's Cookshop* and going on yearly trips to the USA and Europe to buy unique cookware for the store. I was incredibly lucky to be able to develop my passion, personality and style in this way.

After several years in the homewares industry, sourcing and procuring products from Taiwan, Korea, Europe and the USA, it was time again for me to make a change. I was married to a wonderful man, Tony, and all was going well. For the first time in my life I had financial support, yet I missed the world of performing arts and wanted to return to my original passions.

A move into arts management

The change meant reinventing the performing artist in me into a management career and I started by running the *Bartuccio Dance Studio*, where I gained enormous experience in the area of commercial dance: supplying dancers for fashion parades, television, advertisements, movies and stage shows.

Then, in 1988, I moved into my dream job as Corporate Development Manager at The Australian Ballet. I remember achieving some extraordinary feats in this role. For example, I spent three months in London putting together the ballet's Royal Gala, where Princess

Diana was in attendance. These were some of the happiest times in my life: I was living in a chic Covent Garden hotel; my office was in the magnificent building of the Victorian Consul General; I jogged daily past the Royal Opera House and other beautiful and historical parts of London. Life was good. I was far away from the challenges of my personal life – and this gave me some respite – yet I knew that I'd soon go back to Melbourne and have to face up to a crumbling marriage and take stock of my career.

After this brief but joyful interlude I returned to Melbourne. The year was 1992 and though I loved my job I was exhausted from travelling and the burden of business problems in my husband's life, so at the age of 43 I resigned from The Australian Ballet. This was challenging, although deep down I knew that I had to sort myself out psychologically – until then I'd been able to mask my emotional hurts and disappointments behind my job.

I desperately needed time-out to think about how I would move forward in my life. I knew I'd been band-aiding parts of myself together. I saw a psychiatrist who helped me with the move from the ballet, my failing marriage and, following a disastrous real estate investment, the collapse of my financial security. I felt alone and for the first time in my life I didn't know what I wanted to do. All I knew was that I had to keep working on myself psychologically or else fall in a heap.

Mind, meditation and personal growth

I'd always been interested in the mind, meditation and personal growth and, over the next few months, I began to gain clarity on the direction my career should take. In 1995 I decided to study psychotherapy and, as I wanted to stay in the arts world and also enjoy the challenge of mixing with smart business leaders, the path became clear: my next business would contain programs and coaching where there was an intersection of business and creative thinking for senior executives and their teams.

I enrolled in Soul Centred Psychotherapy training in St Kilda, Melbourne and spent the next four years in intense training. I was amongst people who weren't part of the performing arts or business world. It was a shock since it seemed that these people spoke a different language. I had to learn to become part of this new world of psychotherapy and personal growth – a world where without the arts to escape to, I was exposed. I'd rather have fundraised millions of dollars than be put through some of the confronting personal learning that made up this training but I knew it was essential for my psychological growth and future role as an executive coach.

Psychotherapy training was the most personally challenging time of my life. I could have jumped ship, yet I knew that I must do the hard yards. I was emotionally drained after all the life and business problems that resulted from the loss of Tony's property business. And so it was a case of, *'Knuckle down and do this',* or else be an unhappy and unfulfilled woman for the rest of my life.

During my training, every emotion and feeling that I'd tried to hide through the years was exposed. I was stripped bare yet had nowhere to run because we had to understand our own *'shit'* before we could work with clients. I remember looking at the group and thinking, *'What am I doing here? I want to wear my heels and beautiful clothes again.'* But underneath I knew I couldn't face the corporate world yet. I needed a sabbatical.

And yes, I learnt that there was a big part of me, ashamedly, who thought herself above others. I had worked hard and achieved great results – so *'look at me, look at me!'* But that didn't happen with the group at the Kairos Centre. Here, I had to confront my demons and consciously understand damaging psychological patterns so that these behaviours didn't have a stranglehold over me as I moved along a path of transformation.

I spent part of 1997 in the USA at Esalen Institute in Big Sur, California. This experience helped me to understand myself in a creative and insightful way. People of all ages came from around the world to this magical place to practice Zen meditation, dance, move, and grow. Above all, they came to experience the healing arts program that features the Esalen Massage – reputedly the best massage treatment in the world. Massage tables are on a deck high above the coastline of Big Sur, with hot tubs below. Pure bliss.

My year in the USA also included several months in Boulder, Colorado, amongst the magnificent Rocky Mountains. I attended the Naropa University Buddhist summer school, enrolling in the Jack Kerouac Summer Writing program and studying Jungian dream work. I ended my year in the USA with three months in Santa Fe living in the Upaya Zen Centre. Joan Halifax was the Roshi and a wonderful teacher in practical applications for Zen practise in life.

During this year I learnt to build resilience and trust my inner-sense of self. Though at the ballet I felt I was invincible, I had suffered a loss of confidence since leaving. Here, I learnt not to get caught up in the trappings of success or even the teachings of gurus and instructors. (Life happens. Shit happens. People are challenged – even those we put on pedestals. And it is precisely because they have been wounded by challenges that they are able to help us through ours.) Looking internally rather than externally for inspiration and self-belief was a steep learning curve, and forms part of the foundation of this book.

When I returned to Melbourne and finished my psychotherapy training, I was ready to start working again though this too was confronting. My high-achiever gene told me I could simply set-up shop with a creative coaching program, yet this did not turn out to be the case. I had to learn how to set up a sustainable business model using creative thinking and move back into my passion for music in a whole new way. I constructed the initial program on my own – the self-reliant sits well within me!

Founding Corporate Creative Directions

In 2002 Tony died from prostate cancer. Though we'd divorced several years previously, his death prompted me to move to Byron Bay where I felt I'd be energetically supported, and that all my business plans would fall into place. I knew I must create a career path that inspired and gave my life meaning (as well as financial security). However, I began to realise that I needed to put this program into a format that business people would understand.

Though the name of the program *Corporate Creative Directions* was born, and my good friend Luella put the copy together on my methodology, the website went live and then not much happened. I thought I'd be travelling regularly from Byron to run my coaching and training programs in Sydney and Melbourne – but I learned from a well-respected friend and CEO that I hadn't a hope in hell getting it running from Byron. If I was to get things moving, he said, I must return to Melbourne.

So in 2008 I sold my home in Byron Bay and came back to Melbourne. (In hindsight I should have done this earlier as I loved being back in this great city.) I set about getting *Corporate Creative Directions* (CCD) up and running, resurrecting old networks and setting up new ones, which was tough initially. However, once I'd put the time and resources into birthing CCD in Melbourne, it took off.

The lessons I've learnt have been enormous and I believe that through journeying this path, I can help you move through the maze of your Work–Life challenges.

There's no one better to guide you in life than someone who has been there before.

As a business coach, I work with executives in the areas of Work Life Balance and career reinvigoration, helping clients unlock their creative mindset to solve their personal and professional challenges.

So, after reading my story, start to imagine how you could reinvent your life when faced with change, change that takes you into new areas of your life path, areas that ignite the passionate woman within …

How to use this book

In each chapter there will be questions and exercises to reflect upon and answer. These will ignite the flame, internally connecting the true 'You' to those passions, talents, skills and achievements that you may have forgotten.

This will begin to bring together an unearthing and development of your next stage. It will help in several ways to reinvigorate your career, by bringing new thinking and intuition into your professional and personal life.

Throughout the coming chapters, I'll continue to remind you of the enormous creative, insightful potential that you have hidden within. I call it the *gold* and I want you to find access to it hidden in your vault. Go within, find the combination, and connect with your inner wisdom that resides there. We all have this place within and yours will help you create your own encore.

Questions

Don't over think these questions – just write, and don't let the perfectionist try to correct your grammar and punctuation. A good trick is to use pen and paper and not take the pen off the page until you're finished. What you're doing at this stage is setting the framework for the rest of the book. Enjoy.

1. Write a brief outline of your life – a page is sufficient.
2. What parts of your career do you love?
3. What parts of your personal life do you love?
4. What is challenging in your career at present?
5. What is challenging in your personal life at present?

About You

Creating your life story scripts

Now that you have read my story, I'd love you to put together a couple of your own. The first one is your story until now and the second is your story 10 years from now.

As a woman of 40+, I imagine that you've had a rather interesting and perhaps challenging life. Now is the time to let it all out. The telling of your story is for you only – it's not necessary to share your story with others – and this experience, in itself, is empowering and cathartic. It's about having the courage to tell your story as it truly is. I know this to be true from my own experience. I was told for nearly 20 years to write a book about my life – its challenges and its fabulous times – yet I could not put a sentence together that sounded authentic until now.

Did you know that we somehow forget much of our life's challenges and successes? I'm constantly asking clients to tell me more about their achievements, yet it's like amnesia happens around these experiences! Aren't we meant to celebrate them and include these 'wins' in our life's story? Of course we are! Most women forget times when they've had success, yet when they dig deep they find that these stories are powerful and important reminders of what they've achieved. Be reminded of your 'gold star' moments and reframe your challenges with new eyes; recall long forgotten resources that worked for you; inspire yourself so that you can move into challenging situations with confidence. These methods worked in the past – do not forget them.

I remember a challenge that a coaching client faced several years ago. She was a woman in her 50s and a high-level business leader. She had achieved great career success and wanted to climb further up the ladder. However, she felt that younger staff members were making her doubt her strong business skills and background. I asked my client to write her life story and I was quite astounded when she shyly handed me her notes. The woman sitting in front of me did not resemble the woman in the story. The woman sitting in front of me was tired, exhausted, had lost her passion and purpose, and had a lack of self-belief. She reminded me of a trapped animal, not knowing where to turn or how to escape a dangerous situation.

When we transcribed all her career highlights onto one page, my client was amazed – there were so many reports and articles on her successes that she had 'conveniently' forgotten. We worked on her behavioural challenges which helped her to understand how and why she reacted to situations when feeling threatened. This was a significant turning point in her life and I saw a spark and the lights go on in her eyes. It was fantastic! Several months later this client told me that, at that moment, she had finally become aware of the part of her that could sabotage the successful woman, and that now she was alert to this behavioural pattern, she was able to take steps to prevent it from making her feel inadequate, especially when challenged.

What happened in putting her story together was that the block she had put up around life achievements was exposed. Following this we were able to work on ways to change this behaviour pattern. This situation is common – many clients forget their achievements. It can result from peer group pressure as we grow up when we're encouraged to 'not stand out too much' or challenged by the question, *'Who do you think you are?'* In response to this we suppress our wins with words resonating deeply within us such as, *'This win was a surprise. Am I really smarter than the others, and do I really have the talent to keep moving ahead?'*

I find it really sad that for many people success is not a cause for celebration. And, yes, until my 40s successes were pushed to the back of my mind too. Unconsciously I didn't want to show myself as the high-achieving woman I was. When I made, or had forced upon me, the need to make a career and life change in my 40s, I entered a different world – a new world of friends who supported me regardless of what happened in my life; friends who would come round to my house with gourmet treats and a bottle of wine. I learned how to acknowledge and celebrate my successes, rather than moving straight onto the next challenge. I realised the importance of celebrating small wins and of reciprocating and acknowledging my friend's successes too.

Writing your life story script

Writing your story can be transforming – both personally and professionally. I suggest that you lock yourself away in a quiet place and start writing. Handwriting your story rather than using a computer is best since putting pen to paper is a positive kinesthetic way of getting in touch with the real 'You'. A great tip is to not take your pen off the paper for 10 minutes – and just write. When you do this you're able to stop your critical censor entering into the story – the part of you that can jeopardise the true 'You' being heard. Write your story in 10-minute blocks. Do it in one go, if possible, as the energy must keep moving forward. When you've finished, read the story but do not edit. This is not for publication – this is *your* story and I imagine you'll be amazed at what you have written.

There will be parts of your life that you've forgotten – success and challenges. The unfolding of your story is a bit like the television show from many years ago, *This Is Your Life*. Do you remember how the subject was overwhelmed and exhilarated as colleagues and friends recalled significant events from their past? It's amazing how much we pack into our lives! I know that when I wrote my story for psychotherapy training many years ago, I felt humbled as I remembered parts of my life that I'd forgotten – particularly the achievements. I was amazed at what I had accomplished.

As you read this you may be telling yourself that you've nothing worthwhile to write about. This is common with many women and I imagine it's not true. All you need to do is to get the first significant parts of your life out on paper.

Perhaps you'll unearth, as my client did, an understanding of behavioural patterns from the past that are not serving you now. This is the *gold* – the uncovering of coping mechanisms that may well have been around for many years. You can now become aware that they are outdated and can interfere when conflict happens. Once you get the 'ah-ha' moment of revelation, their power over you is diminished. You can move forward in your life. It's liberating.

What's developing in this chapter is a creative way to re-engage with the woman you truly are. Creativity adds another dimension to our lives. When we tell our story, we connect with our internal self and a world of possibilities; the part of us, (recognised and embraced by performing artists), that creates flow and joy in our lives, not just on the concert stage – but also in our workplace and at home.

Writing your life story script 10 years from now

The next story to write is in answer to the question, *'In a perfect world, with nothing to stop you, where will you be and what will you be doing in 10 years' time?'*

Before starting your story, I suggest that you put on some music that inspires you, whether your preferred style is classical, jazz, rock, lounge or otherwise. Become the director of your show. Let your imagination run wild. Do not censor your writing. Write for 10 minutes without taking your pen off the paper. Stop and keep going for another 10 minutes. Just be mad, creative, outrageous. Let whatever is inside of you come out.

When you've finished, keep the music playing and read what you have written. I imagine that you will feel alive, inspired and energised by this act of writing. Your story will contain some powerful information that will help move your career and personal life forward in a more fulfilling direction. Your story might even include some unconventional ideas, and that's great! There are ways to leverage this inspirational thinking into workable parts of your life, and in the chapter on creative thinking you'll find examples from my life and more.

Now, if you're feeling exhilarated by the exercise, you may want to put this fun piece of writing together. I was inspired by this concept when I saw a movie recently, a smart screenplay and very funny. The main character, a woman in her 40s, suffers a head injury in a car accident. When she comes out of a coma she is her teenage self, however, she still retains her 40-year-old knowledge and is therefore able to live as her younger self with the benefits of her life experience. She becomes a leader of her school peers and prevents friends moving into relationships that will not work. She can do this because she has access to past memories. The question for you is this, *'If you knew what you know now, what would you change as you grew up?'*

I suggest you write one page about how you would live your life as a teenager now. Go back into your past using your life experience from today. What changes? Perhaps your school years would be different, or where you lived. Have fun with this exercise. What this is doing is building up the creative 'You' – getting ideas, thoughts, concepts and passions out of your head and onto paper.

When I first did this exercise, some of the awareness that came up was that I would have gone to a performing arts school; that it would have been in Paris; I would have spent heaps of time at concerts; eating great food (especially cheese); I would have had a number of handsome French boyfriends. It would have been a lot different to growing up in Christchurch, New Zealand!

Over the next days and weeks, keep going back to read the stories you have written. In doing so, you will create a foundation from your own life experiences that will support your creative growth – and you will find new ways to inspire yourself to reach your true potential. Your stories are like a feast. Let your feast nourish you.

Finding Your Support Team

When we go through changes in our life, we must be prepared for this: well meaning friends and colleagues will see a sassy, savvy, upbeat woman emerge – and this may challenge them. They might like to follow your path but do not have the courage – it's as simple as that.

There can be a million and one excuses why they can't do what you're doing – and some of their excuses will be valid. However, this is about the next stage of *your* life, and it will drive home some truths about you and the people around you, even though many of those who challenge you will be long-standing friends.

In the years since I turned 40 and went on this journey, friends and family have questioned me about what I was doing. Sometimes it was as if it were a competition or a test. *'So, what have you achieved so far?'* It was as if I had to report in on where my life was going.

I remember, when I left the ballet and started studying psychotherapy, I found that some of my closest friends questioned me like a school principal about why I was going down this path. At the time I didn't realise that this was about *them*, and *their* discomfort around personal development. For example, for some of my friends it was easier to stay in an unfulfilling marriage. They would say to me, '*How will I survive financially if I leave my husband?*' And then they would have affairs to satisfy their sexual needs. It was as if they were living double lives.

At the start of the change I was also quite conflicted. I knew deep down that I was meant to be doing this, yet I had no job or career path mapped out. As a woman who from the age of 12 had worked during the school holidays and had always found waitressing or cleaning jobs during university, I realised that I was out on a precipice. And although I had no idea where I was going to end up, I kept holding onto the slim belief that I would use this psychotherapy training to help me take my musical passions back into the corporate world.

I was also mixing with a totally different group of people. I still remember walking into the room on the first day of psychotherapy training. I had to do a double take: this gathering resembled a hippy tribe, whereas I'd come from the corporate world of Chanel suits and French champagne. Yet something inside me said, '*You have to go ahead. You have to take your life to the next level. But first you must understand yourself and find a way to leverage this knowledge into your new creative coaching work.*'

Of the people I met in training, two women have become life-long friends and members of my support team.

My support team

There are three special women in my life who are my support team – Carmel, Arian and Ivana. We've known each other for over 15 years and have shared both highs and lows. During this time we've all been there for each other, encouraging, supporting and challenging each other in positive ways.

I met Ivana at the Sydney Opera House when we played in the orchestra for The Australian Opera and Ballet. She had fled from Prague in 1968 during the Russian invasion and, though she had no simple English, we spoke the same language – the language of music. We were close then and became closer over the years, even when our lives took different paths – hers as a mother, mine as a career woman. I believe that her life's challenges, though very different, enabled her to support me through mine.

I came to meet my other friends, Carmel and Arian, at psychotherapy training. We were all from very different backgrounds: Arian is a former Buddhist nun who has a rich and full life; Carmel has a social work and aged-care background. Their friendship and support is priceless to me and they are still my closest friends. I believe our friendship has survived because we saw each other expose our fears and insecurities, and we worked through them together.

I wonder how many friends and family members stay with us through our challenges? It's a bit like a marriage – it will survive if you see and accept even the worst of your partner. I now look at my friends and family thinking,

'Thank goodness I was able to learn about myself, and not have to pretend to be someone I am not.'

I imagine that if you're reading this book, you want to change too and move ahead in your life. Certainly, there will be times when the path you've chosen will reach a dead end – then you must return to the creative part of you and find another path that connects.

I must add that you'll be fine. I know that when we have the courage to move into a new stage of our life, things happen and the challenge is that the way forward may not appear in a structured way, but instead, appear randomly. It's like putting together the pieces of a jigsaw puzzle – at times there will be heaps of blue sky and you think to yourself, *'How does that fit together?'* Then *'Bingo!'* A piece with a flying bird appears and helps you put that final part of the jigsaw together.

Some suggestions to help you move along this path

- Always keep in mind what life was like before the change, and how life is now.
- Always remember the question in the introduction, *'Do I want to look back on my life in 10 years and find that I'm stuck in the same unfulfilling career or relationship?'*
- Always have one or two really close friends who understand why you wanted to turn your life around. Try to have people who come from a neutral position, rather than those you work with. Special friends are those who listen, have lived an unconventional life and

importantly understand themselves. They are a rare breed – take care that they don't fly away, or become extinct.

I believe that when we have the support of special friends we can climb the highest mountain and let our inspiring woman out. She has always been there. With your special friends supporting you, now is the time to set her free.

Mindset

From my experience in the arts world I know only too well, that mindset can make or break a performance. It's the same with difficult life situations: our minds control how we deal with challenges and our perception of the world.

Put simply, our thought patterns control how strong or weak we feel, helping us move through challenges when we have a positive mindset or contributing to our failure if we look at a challenge through negative eyes.

I've used the following exercise hundreds of times with clients and groups and it never fails to prove the power of positive and negative thoughts on our body.

A fun exercise to show the power of negative and positive mindset

(You'll need to find someone to do this with.)

1. Hold your right arm out in front of you and think a negative thought.
2. Have your partner push down on your arm.
3. Your arm is weak and gives in. This blocked energy is due to negative thoughts.

4. Now try it with your left arm held straight out in front.
5. Stay with the same negative thought.
6. The result will be the same.
7. Now try again holding your right arm in front of you and think a positive thought.
8. See what magic happens? Your arm is still holding strong!
9. Now try it with your left arm and see how it works again.

A strong mindset wins the race

A great example where positive mindset is used to achieve optimum results is in the world of the elite athlete. When I ran creative programs at the Institute of Sport, a coach told me that there can be two athletes who have the same potential to win a race but pitted against each other, it's the athlete with the strongest mindset that wins. Musicians use the same mindset techniques to create performances of excellence.

Through my work with athletes and musicians I also became aware of the importance of first creating a vision, following this through with a training plan with the icing on the cake being a positive mindset. This process forms the foundation of my programs and this book.

Find the courage to confront old mindset patterns and discover a whole new world

I recently coached a young musician who suffered performance anxiety. I'd heard her play and she was very talented. It was clear that the problem was not her ability, but rather, her mindset.

Since I work a lot in this area I was able to help her quickly and effectively. When asked about her fears she admitted she had doubts about her performance so I continued to unpack her mindset to find out where this lack of self-belief came from. We soon got to the core of the problem – she wanted to please her parents and stand out from fellow students. (This answer is common in the performing arts and business world – it doesn't matter if you're standing on stage or at the front of a boardroom.)

My client was using old coping mechanisms that were well known to her. They ranged from one extreme to another and included Perfectionism coupled with her desire to be accepted by fellow peers, creating Confusion and Self-Sabotage. By giving in to the negative dialogue in her head she had a 'way out' if her performance was not up to standard. Projection was also at play as she blamed external events on her performance.

Most of our coping mechanisms have been around us for many years and may have kept us safe when we were growing up. For example, if we don't stand out from the others at school then we'll fit in. And because the brain is like intersecting pathways that we travel along regularly when we stick to the same route each day, nothing changes. So too when we try to solve challenges in the same old way – we get stuck and afraid of moving into new thinking. But when we set off on another path we find a whole new landscape appears. Start thinking differently and try a new path, and it will bring us new vision and solutions.

After only three sessions my client understood how her thinking was causing her performance anxiety. When she was stressed before a performance she went back along the same path thinking, *'I'm not good enough, I will stuff up this performance.'* The challenge for her was to reframe the old negative thinking to, *'I will perform brilliantly because I am a talented musician.'* This approach worked and I had a wonderful call from her after a performance to tell me that she'd come second in a big music competition. She'd never received such great results! I was thrilled for her. She was very talented; it was her mind that was getting in the way.

The hardest part in developing a positive mindset is uncovering how past challenges have contributed to the presenting problem or negative mindset pattern. Bringing a client to conscious awareness of how they use old coping mechanisms that self-sabotage a solving of the problem creates the 'ah-ha' moment of clarity. Reframing the challenge in light of this new knowledge is the birth of a positive mindset. This strategy then becomes an essential part of the client's toolbox and they know that when difficult situations arise they mustn't let old negative psychological patterns stop the reframing process.

The development of a positive mindset can be likened to building a beautiful home. If the foundations (the conscious awareness of old negative patterns) are not secure, the house will have structural problems forever.

The house may stay up but other sections of the house will become weakened due to lack of solid foundations.

Challenges and anxieties in the corporate world are almost identical. There's a sense of, *'What if I stuff up?'* and, *'Do I really have the expertise to present this information?'* Even the smartest insights can go pear-shaped when we doubt ourselves.

This is an area that I've had to work on personally for many years. There can be days when I'm feeling a bit flat and coupled with this my self-belief goes out the window. I now have a way of dealing with this part of myself: instead of getting swept up by these feelings, I challenge it and tell it that it has no control over me now. By doing this I dilute the pull of my mindset. I also try not to dwell on the challenge, which can become as big as a mini-series if I let it.

Some things to remember
- You are the master of your knowledge. You would not be an executive woman without enormous knowledge and ability. This is one point to get – and I mean *really* get!
- Self-doubt can arise from being unfulfilled in personal and professional life, so what are you going to do to change this?
- Don't be the scapegoat. If people around you are unhappy or challenging, it's about them not you.

It's very easy, as women, to think that we are the cause of others unhappiness. I excelled in this thinking: wanting to solve other people's challenges so I'd be liked and loved.

When you have the courage to put your beliefs and values forward, how do others hear you? Are they supportive or challenging? Again, this thought pattern, which stems from childhood, is very familiar to me – many times when I dared to have my own point of view or question my parents I wasn't heard or I was dismissed.

Challenges often come from those who are experts in criticism. When someone puts his or her dissatisfaction or blame onto you, this behaviour is known as Projection. This blame comes from their internal fear and self-doubt – it's far easier to blame you. These people need to take responsibility for their own dissatisfaction.

There's a saying that rings true, *'There are people so unhappy with their life that they'd be unhappy even in Paradise.'*

Think about this for a moment.
- Be aware of what you say to yourself when something goes wrong. Do you tell yourself that you were stupid, or an idiot? A great way to reframe this language is to ask yourself, *'Would I use this language to a close friend?'* I imagine you wouldn't.
- Give yourself some distance from the challenge. Instead of standing on top of it, take several steps back (you might even walk into another room or space). This is so that your emotions are less involved.

- Keep re-writing your life story. Include all your personal and professional experience. Write new versions every month. By the time you've written your story several times, instead of underselling or forgetting your achievements as you may do at the start, I'm sure you'll be thrilled at your achievements.
- When you're feeling challenged, ask yourself the following questions:
  › Is this a situation that occurs regularly?
  › Why do I keep responding this way?
  › Is this the way I've always responded to threats through my life? This question is the *gold* as it gives you information leading to the core of *why your mindset does what it does*.
- The key to turning around negative mindset patterns is to stay conscious when threatened. Only when you recognise these patterns can you change them.

When confronted with fear it's a normal defence mechanism to use the survival skills that our mind has developed through years of responding to fearful situations. This idea was highlighted to me during psychotherapy training. I was an expert at splitting off from challenges, I'd go vague and not remember what was said. The key is to stay conscious while the challenge is occurring. Breathe – and then reframe the challenge immediately. This will bring some relief and a way of moving forward.

For example, if you're feeling challenged by the

approach you've taken in putting a new program together and fellow peers are questioning you on its validity, put a positive spin on the situation by saying to yourself, *'I understand this program and know it will work,'* rather than, *'Maybe this program will not work. I am a failure.'*

Calmly find a way to truly believe that, *'I can create a workshop that's successful.'* Do not become a victim. Tell yourself that you can't sort out the entire challenge in this meeting and that you'll go away and think about it. Give yourself some space and the opportunity to step back from the emotional feelings that can destroy rational thinking. This will allow you to quietly work on a solution or answers that support your expertise. I applaud people who can say, *'Honestly I don't have the answers at this moment. I will go away and come back with them.'*

What you're doing is giving yourself time to separate from the same response pattern to mindset challenges that you've had for years. Remember the exercise that I suggested at the start of the chapter and how weak our body can become when we think negative thoughts? It's important to know that the way your mind reacts to these situations will diminish, so too the fear and anxiety. These are old coping mechanisms that do not serve you well any more.

As you move towards an understanding of your mindset, you can find out why you still put up with these challenges in your life. Is it time for you to begin thinking about a new career direction? Or do you want to visualise your present job with new eyes?

An introduction to a most important tool - meditation

I want to give you an important tool and resource in this chapter of the book – an introduction to meditation. When I learnt to meditate many years ago it changed my life. Meditation calms your mind, makes you more peaceful and able to move through challenges.

You can start off meditating for 10 minutes and then build up to longer periods. Or do a couple of short meditation sessions during the day. It will be one of your best tools for creating a more balanced life.

I suggest you record the script below onto your phone, iPad or laptop. Read the script very slowly, pausing every few seconds.

Breath meditation

Take some time to become comfortable on a chair or on the floor. Let the sounds around you go into the background.

As you become more comfortable, you will be aware of your breath moving through your body. On the inhale, visualise your breath moving up though the tip of your nose and going deep into your body, replenishing and nourishing all the cells in your body. And then on the out breath coming back down through your nostrils, out of your body. If any thoughts come up don't become attached to them, imagine them drifting away like a balloon into the sky. Just stay with this breathing, becoming aware of your body relaxing into this simple meditation. If you get distracted you may like to count as you inhale and count as you exhale, keeping the counting equal with both the inhale and the exhale.

After 10 minutes slowly bring your attention back into the room by moving your fingers, hands, legs and the rest of your body.

With regular practise you'll find this meditation will help you to become more relaxed.

Use it at work and at home:
- At the start of the day
- Before an important meeting
- When you're feeling tired or stressed
- When you have difficulty concentrating
- As a reviver at lunch time
- On planes, in taxis, if you travel frequently for work
- At night when you return home.

Get acquainted with the Work-Life Balance Wheel

As businesswomen, we're very good at multi-tasking. Many of my clients tell me how they have a routine each workday. One woman said that her young children know it's the weekend when she comes down the stairs wearing jeans.

Executive working life is about being able to balance stress and feel fulfilled in all areas. However, as we know, striking this balance is notoriously hard to do. Fortunately, there are many techniques you can learn to help you with and through your stress. This is why the topic of Work–Life Balance is one of my most popular workshops and coaching programs.

As we move into our 40s and beyond, I believe that we have the opportunity to be open-minded and resolute about our priorities in regard to both personal and professional life. There's never been a better time to be honest with ourselves and create a more fulfilling and less stressful life. It mustn't be at the expense of endless long hours in our workplace – many women need to say '*no*' to after-hours commitments and not worry that it will make their careers vulnerable.

My struggle with Work-Life Balance

I am reminded of the time when I left The Australian Ballet. I loved every part of my job as head of the Corporate Development Department: finding corporate funds; hosting events; travelling. All these tasks made me feel alive and successful. I was at the gym most nights and life was good until one day I had an anxiety attack while watching a theatre performance – and this continued to happen on several more occasions.

After a few months of suffering these anxiety attacks I knew that I had to change my life. My marriage was challenged (my husband's business had been through major financial problems); I lived between two homes (Sydney and Melbourne); I had the job of my dreams yet there was very little balance in my life. Finally, I made the difficult decision to leave the ballet.

I still remember the day I left. It was Christmas 1993. I was sad to leave this wonderful organisation yet, as I left and walked by myself towards St Kilda beach, I felt like a weight had been lifted off my shoulders both personally and professionally.

On reflection, if I knew what I know now, I'd have approached my working life very differently. I may not have left my career at the ballet if I'd been familiar with the techniques I'll be sharing with you in this book. I was a person who needed to be in control and I didn't know

Creating Encores

how to ask for help. If I'd had ways to understand my feelings, emotions and behaviours I may have set upon a different path.

I now know that I had the Perfectionist driver within me and this is a characteristic that many of my coaching clients share. I found it hard to show my fears and weaknesses because I wanted the world to see what I could achieve. (This part stems from having to prove myself as a child and over-achieve in order to be seen and loved.) The Perfectionist driver can make me rather overpowering in some situations yet she has many positive sides too: she helps me work hard; cook great food; go to the gym; look my best; develop special friendships and so on.

Moving through this tough time has given me the authentic personal experience to allow me to support women in finding balance in their lives. Indeed for some, my help may prevent them from leaving fulfilling careers. Are you in a career that you love yet have challenges that threaten to derail you?

You the Director

Imagine you are the director of your own show. What's the name of your production? Where will you stage it? How will you cast it? Who will create the sets, lighting, costumes, music and choreography? You must work all of this out before you can *get this show on the road*. This chapter, a prelude to the visioning chapters, is like the research stage of your up-coming production.

About the Work-Life Balance Wheel

The Wheel is a diagnostic tool that shows the different areas of your personal and professional life. It reveals where you excel and which areas require work.

Before you move into the Work–Life Balance Wheel spend a few minutes reflecting on yourself honestly. *Who am I?* Start to notice the thoughts, the feelings that arise. *Where am I in my life?* Are you ready to move ahead into a new stage of your business life or do you want to leverage your skills and pull back from life in the fast lane? By moving through the Work–Life Balance Wheel you'll find clarity about your life as it is now. There will be a few 'ah-ha' moments that shine a light on your Work–Life patterns. The following chapters will then help you with methodology to open stuck or out of balance sections of The Wheel.

There are eight sections in The Wheel, each of these relates to part of your life. There will be sections that aren't in balance and this is normal. Become acquainted with these parts of your life. The visual diagram is proof of where action is required. The *gold* to finding Work–Life Balance is to connect with the areas that are out of balance.

The eight sections of The Wheel:

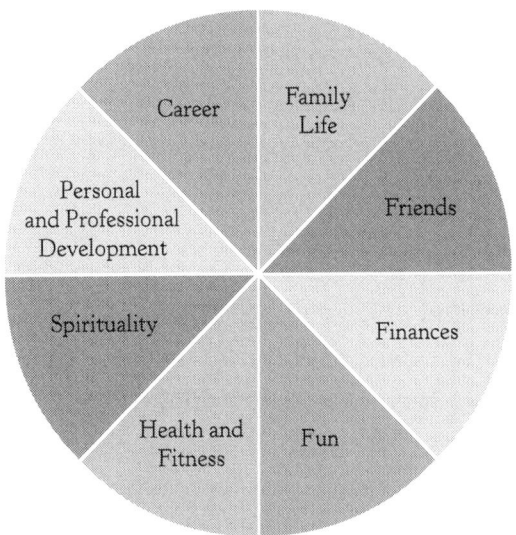

What does The Wheel mean to you?

This activity will give you insight and clarity.

1. Connect with and rate each section of The Wheel from 1–10. (One means you feel totally out of balance or challenged in that area. 10 means you feel in balance.) Write the lower numbers near the centre of the circle and the higher numbers towards the edge of the circle. For example, if your Career isn't quite as you want it, you may rate it five as there's room for improvement. However, if you're smart with money, save and invest wisely and feel that Finance is one of the areas you're

most proud of, you may rate this section a nine. Spend five minutes on each.

2. When you've scored each of the sections, draw a line between each section and see the shape of your wheel. Is it a beautiful Michelin tyre or does it look like a prehistoric, roughly-fashioned wooden wheel that is not going to get you very far?

What you have now is an understanding of your life, both personally and professionally. There will be sections of the Work–Life Balance Wheel where you feel life is going along well and needs only a little improvement. There will be other areas that need substantial help. Perhaps you have wanted to change these areas but other challenges got in the way. Perhaps they were put in the 'too hard' basket. Remember the lower scoring sections are the *gold* for it's when you turn these sections around that you'll create a more fulfilling and less stressful life path.

> *'Over a number of years there's been a tiny stone in your shoe. Initially it irritated a part of your foot and you tried to remove it, but couldn't. Or the stone was so small that you couldn't be bothered stopping and removing it. You put up with it. Over the years you and your foot became used to the uncomfortable tiny stone. Perhaps forgetting it was even there. The day that you find the stone and remove it you wonder how ever you put up with the discomfort.'*

For example, in considering the Fun section, you may have told yourself that there was no time to let go and enjoy life. Maybe your career and bringing up a family took up every spare minute. I suggest my clients give themselves permission to see a comedy, read a lighthearted book, go out with girlfriends, to laugh and take time out. I tell myself this when I get too serious about Life and Work, and a comedy at the movies always hits the mark. I come out feeling like a new woman, wondering how I could let myself get so serious about parts of my life. I know from my own and client's experiences that low scoring sections of The Wheel need to be turned around to prevent them having power over you.

The scoring system from each part of The Wheel creates an 'ah-ha' moment of realisation.

There is no escaping this information.

Gaining more clarity around your Work-Life Balance

Here are some more questions that will help to create understanding and growth towards new ways of developing your Work–Life Balance.

Career

At this stage of your life you deserve to be going along a career path that lights you up, inspires you and which every day has you looking forward to the challenges and inspiration it brings.

Ask yourself:
- Am I in a career I love?
- Does my career fulfil me?
- If I had to work in my career for zero salary would I? This question is both challenging and confirming.

Rate this section 1–10

I suggest that as you do this, you create a picture of your career at present. See yourself in your work environment and the people around you. Go into the energy in your workplace, the sounds around you too. Now watch yourself impartially, doing whatever it is that you do.

If your career is one that fulfils you, you'll have no problem answering these questions. If it does not fulfil you, your score will tell you. It will be low.

And if you've been putting up with a career half-lived so far, this section of the Work–Life Balance Wheel will encourage you to think seriously about finding a career path that inspires. Maybe it's about taking time to ask yourself, *'Why did I move into this career?'* and, *'How can I find a way to leverage my skills and passions in another direction?'*

With each section of The Wheel I suggest that you trust your inner wisdom. Give the internal 'You' permission to ask, *'Do I want to be on this career path for another 10 years or is it time to look at a new career path that excites?'*

Family and home life

Ask yourself:

- How important is my family?
- What type of connection do I have with my parents and siblings?
- Even if they are not close by, do I still feel a connection?
- What was my family life like growing up? Were my parents supportive?
- Do we give to each other as an ideal family would?
- Has my childhood family experience helped me to live the life I do now, or have I had to work through some

family challenges?

- Do I support my family? Do they support me?
- How does my family fit into my work life?
- Am I able to successfully combine motherhood and my career?
- How connected am I to my children, husband or partner and what does this mean to me?

Move on to these questions about the home you live in:

- Is my home a place that exudes warmth and character?
- Does my home welcome me when I walk in the door?
- How important is it to me to have a home that's a space to rest and feel supported?
- Have I been putting up with dysfunctional areas, like a badly designed kitchen or bathroom? Does my home need a bit of a make over?
- How important is it to me to make the outdoor area appealing?

Rate this section 1–10

Our homes are a refuge and a space to relax and recharge our batteries yet we often put up with areas that need some attention. If this sounds like you then start with little steps towards making your home more inviting. Hang a painting; add new lighting or a cushion here and there; tidy up the garden; create a courtyard – you'll appreciate looking at it in the winter and sitting there in the summer months.

Friends

Ask yourself:

- How important are friendships to me?
- Do I have many long-term friendships?
- What do these connections mean to me?
- Am I able to move through challenges of friendships and not walk away?
- What do I love about my friends?
- What do I imagine they love about me?

Rate this section 1–10

I know that I learnt more about myself when I started psychotherapy training with a new group of people. It taught me to look more closely at past friendships and ask myself, *'Did I give to my friends or did I put them on the back burner as I was too busy working or travelling?'*

When my life went pear-shaped in my 40s I found out the hard way that I didn't have many close friends – people I could talk to deeply about my fears and challenges; friends who could truly hear me without dismissing my words. I also learnt that to have support from friends I needed to be there for them. I learnt the importance of developing this part of me – the giver. Once I had mastered this important core need of strong friendships, I attracted friends who were true, supportive, loving and caring. I know that they will be there if I need them as I will be for them.

Many of my clients say to me, *'I don't have many friends'*. I explain that as long as you have one or two close friends who are there for you, and vice versa, they are all you need.

If your score is low in this section I encourage you to look deeply within yourself and find some answers to these questions. It may well be about not having time. Then ask yourself, *'How can I resurrect my friendships?'* Start by just giving back to friends, phoning, going out for a meal, a drink or to a show. You'll know what is required.

Finances
Ask yourself:
- What is the current state of my finances?
- Am I smart at balancing business and living expenses?
- Do I charge clients what I am worth?
- What is my cash flow at present?
- Am I a wise investor?
- Do I live from month to month?
- Have I invested time in learning more about smart business finances?
- Have I set aside money for fun, overseas trips, pampering and so on?
- Do I have a sustainable superannuation fund?

Rate this section from 1–10

I could almost guarantee that when I work with clients on the Work–Life Balance Wheel the area of Finance challenges them. Most of my clients want to have greater financial stability and I was one of these people many years ago when I was working long hours; putting myself through university; financing my retail business *Sally's Cookshop*; wondering each week if I'd be able to balance my precarious financial situation. I'm proud to say that I did, and I even made a small profit when I sold my business.

When I married and had the support of two incomes, the fear around finances did move away. Life was good for many years until Tony's business fell apart. Then my 'lacking' mindset around finances came back in full force. I read recently that a wealthy elderly New York woman was challenged financially when she realised that she was down to her last four or five million dollars. This reminded me that we can have strong financial reserves but still feel we're not living an abundant life.

I've now learnt to be grateful for my life, that I have sufficient financial resources for travel, eating out and going to the theatre. I'm smart about living well and have worked on turning around my 'lacking' mentality in regards to finances. I've a well thought out plan that gives me peace of mind and, if the absolute worst happens to me like the share market collapsing again, I can survive and downsize. I remember many years ago seeing a show in London in which the set was a one-bedroom apartment of a woman with fabulous taste. The *pièce de résistance* was a beautiful large ornate gold mirror in the centre of the room. This apartment looked amazing and I said to myself, *'If something beyond my control happens financially I'll replicate this look in an older ornate-style apartment with high ceilings and I'll be very happy.'*

As I grow older the other area connected to my financial portfolio is cultivating the art of giving. This connects with feelings of gratitude and abundance, of being generous. I was at a philanthropy lunch recently and one of the speakers mentioned her early education in giving to others that came from her grandmother. Her grandmother sounded like a special woman who, despite having limited funds, would allocate some of her pension each week to be given to those in need. What a fabulous role model.

My learnings in this area have also come from my friend Carmel who earns a good salary, not large, and who exudes gratitude and generosity. She buys amazing clothes at recycle shops and always looks a million dollars. Whenever she comes to my place for a meal, she brings a quality bottle of wine and other goodies. We eat out at some of Melbourne's hip cool restaurants and we do not go without.

In contrast to Carmel's lifestyle of gratitude there are some people I know who never seem to have enough, even though their assets are triple hers. To me it's all about attitude towards life – the glass is either half full or half empty. I'm so fortunate to have Carmel in my life, she's taught me so much.

I wanted to move you through this section by mentioning my personal experiences in the hope that you can approach the finances section of The Wheel by also asking yourself, '*Do I have enough? Am I happy with what I have and how I spend?*'

I want to finish this section with a comment from a young woman who attended one of my corporate workshops. She had just gone back to work for a legal firm after having her first child. She approached the first stage of visioning with the question, *'In a perfect world, where are you and what are you doing?'* She said she had gone back to work to be able to contribute to an upmarket home. At the end of the visioning program, however, she said that having a large salary was not as important to her as she'd thought. It was more important to have more time with her son. She decided she'd try to find a way to reduce her working hours. Interesting.

You'll now be aware that the Finances section of The Wheel it is not about earning large amounts of money. It's about having an income that can support you with as little stress as possible – a sense of abundance and gratitude combined with a secure financial portfolio.

Fun

Ask yourself:
- When was the last time that I had fun?
- What did I do?
- How often do I schedule in fun days, hours?
- What could I do to let more fun into my life?

Rate this section from 1–10.

I always enjoy working with coaching clients on this section because I'm reminded of the part of me that blossoms and feels alive when I have fun. Too often

I forget to have fun and instead get caught up in my business and life. Yet I know that when I let myself take my life less seriously I feel so much better. The funny part of me comes straight out and I like her very much.

I took the plunge to get in touch with the fun loving part of my life recently. I've always loved burlesque shows – to me they embody the sensual woman that sits within me. The music, the costumes, the moves and WOW the showgirl in me is hooked! I move towards my 'inner gorgeous burlesque woman'.

So there was no stopping me when I saw a burlesque beginners course advertised online. I eagerly enrolled and when the day came I packed my scanty bra tops, short skirts and heels and set off to the class. I arrived at the venue and gasped – it was a very seedy run-down gentleman's club in a dubious part of town. On the window they advertised *Wet T-Shirt Nights*, *Topless Lunches* and much more. I'm no prude, but the joint looked like it should have been demolished. It reeked of suspect men and reminded me of a dark movie set for a variety of illegal practises!

I like to think that I've never been defeated by challenges in my life, so I thought I should at least go inside to check it out. Hanging around outside were some young university students, laughing and also trying to pluck up courage to go inside. Being the oldest I led us inside and what greeted us was worse than I'd imagined: the pole-dancing area was in darkness sending a seedy energy through the space. The carpet was sticky with I dread to think what kind of liquids.

As we walked up to a dressing room we passed a dirty solarium, a filthy toilet hanging off the wall and a notice reading, *'When you have need to go to your car please make sure a security guard accompanies you.'* I was obviously correct about my sense of this place.

We found that our instructor was a very camp guy with tracksuit pants and Ugg boots. So much for the glamour of burlesque! There were plenty of cheap bottles of sparkling wine to assist with confidence that night and, though it didn't inspire me, I was so pleased that I'd had the courage to go up those stairs to the strip club. I never made it to the class performance event several Sunday's later. The thought of performing in that bar area to friends and family was rather incomprehensible to me.

When I look back on those few weeks of burlesque classes they were fun and I have a great story to tell. My 'inner gorgeous burlesque woman' had come out. I may buy a sexy corset and return to classes … but make sure the next course is held in a more glamorous venue!

I often ask my clients, *'Why don't you let yourself have more fun and be happier?'* The reply is often, *'I don't have time.'* As I've mentioned, I'm a culprit too. The 'art of fun' and happiness releases feel-good endorphins in our brain. Great music does this too. There are many ways to engage your 'inner happiness guru' at home too. This can come from creative parts of your life and include:

- Painting
- Cooking interesting food
- Listening to inspiring music

Creating Encores

- Gardening
- Moving, dancing (by moving we release stuck-ness in our body and mind)
- Watching comedy shows
- Reading light-hearted or fantasy books
- Going outside into nature
- Hosting a party (even a lingerie, shoe or Tupperware party!)
- Enrolling in adult learning classes

Whatever your score, promise yourself that you'll find smart ways to make yourself feel more happy and alive. This will keep your stress levels down.

Health and Fitness

Ask yourself:

- How often do I walk or exercise?
- At work do I walk wherever I go or drive or catch a taxi?
- How well do I eat? Truthfully.
- Do I pre-plan meals so that they're delicious and nutritious?
- Am I often exhausted?
- Do I often feel uninspired?
- Do I sleep well?
- How often do I get check-ups with the doctor?
- Do I have a massage or any other pampering treatments regularly?

Rate yourself from 1–10.

This is another essential part of The Wheel. Without a fit and healthy body both career and personal life suffer. I've noticed that fitness is often the first thing to go when we're stressed or working long hours, especially in winter when it's cold, dark and wet. However, I know from my own experience that I feel so much more invigorated, and my limbs seem to have increased lubrication and move more easily. This happens even if I only do a short session at the gym. My head is clearer, and it gets rid of those flat-day blues. Plus it keeps the extra kilos away – important for a woman like me who loves good food and wine! Exercising makes us feel better psychologically as well as physiologically.

When a client of mine started jogging I saw her move from exhaustion into a vibrant woman. As a world-class violinist she travelled constantly and worked irregular hours. I suggested that when she felt a bit flat and tired she should put on her running shoes and go outside. When she did this I could tell – she'd arrive at sessions her face radiant and with a spring in her step. She was a natural runner too.

You can travel easily with a pair of running shoes and it's a great way of getting to know a neighbourhood. When travelling I've found great bars and restaurants, boutiques, shows, and all forms of entertainment by putting on a pair of running shoes and going out for at least 30 minutes.

When we have a fitness regime the health benefits are enormous. Food is fuel (a lesson learnt in my triathlon days) and you start to watch the food that you put into your body. Fitness and health go together especially in a high-level career. You have more energy and feel better within yourself. You can operate at peak level. I wonder if this is why so many people in executive positions train for ironman competitions?

A couple of years ago I found a smart way to increase my intake of healthy food. I organised for a box of fruit and vegetables to be delivered every week. There was no excuse not to cook tasty dishes using the vegetables provided. It also encouraged me to become more creative with food. This is where my love of the recipes of Ottolenghi began, particularly with his book *Plenty* which only has vegetarian dishes using exotic flavours with Middle Eastern spices, herbs and more.

Spirituality

Ask yourself:
- Do I have a regular spiritual practise?
- What do I do to engage inner peace in my life?
- Do I feel exhausted and stressed often?
- Am I constantly rushing from one appointment to the other?
- Do I feel that I am just coping with life?
- Do I feel anxious for no reason?

Rate this section 1–10

This was the part of my life that changed dramatically when I learnt meditation during my early 40s. I was going through challenges in my marriage and remember feeling that I was just about holding my life together. Here I was in a great job working at The Australian Ballet and yet my personal life was falling apart.

The crunch came when I was about to travel to London and seek corporate sponsorship for an upcoming tour. I asked the travel advisor the number of my seat for the flight and it wasn't the one I always had on the aisle. I'm rather ashamed of what happened as I became angry and burst into tears. In a few words, I lost it! I was a mess and was about to get on a plane in a day as the ballet representative. A close friend managed to get me an appointment with a psychologist that day and one of her recommendations was to learn meditation.

This suggestion saved me in so many ways. I learnt to meditate and loved being able to quieten my mind and spend 10 minutes bringing myself back to a more relaxed Sally. It was as if I entered a world of peace and calm. As a hard-core high-achiever I wanted to find out much more about meditation and so I learnt all sorts of advanced techniques which led me towards becoming a new woman – more relaxed, less stressed.

I found many ways to use the calming effects of meditation in my life. Before meetings, going on a plane, even in the toilet at Sydney Opera House! I would sit on the loo seat for 10 minutes and calm myself down with meditation. This moved the part of me that felt overwhelmed by a day and night of functions. Many high-level performing artists use meditation before going

Creating Encores

on stage because it instantaneously relaxes them and takes away their anxiety, leaving them able to create outstanding performances.

Whatever your form of spirituality, having a resource that creates a deep inner sense of peace is priceless. We all have different ways of connecting to this world, whether through formalised religion, or in a variety of spiritual practises.

Ask yourself how your life could be more relaxed and less stressed if you were to learn to meditate? What could you achieve, how would you feel? Remember, meditation is portable. You don't need to be in a special place. All that's required is your ability to tap into silence and quiet within your mind.

Personal and professional development

Personal development
- Am I interested in personal development education?
- Do I dream of having a more satisfying life?
- What is my quality of life like?
- Do I have a value system that's important in life?

Rate this section together with professional development from 1–10

Engaging in personal development gives us a sense of passion and purpose in life. Without it we can live a life that's a bit 'hit or miss'. When you create a personal development plan you must find topics, programs and a path forward that give you a feeling of fulfilment and vitality. It's about following dreams and aspirations. *Do you want to write a book? Live in another country? Develop philanthropic support for others?* It's about forging a path that you can look back on in 10 years and say, *'I achieved those things I set out to do.'* When you're personally fulfilled, work and career challenges become less of a problem. Personal development is generally about you and moves into the area of mind-body understanding.

I know from personal experience that understanding myself has helped me to understand others. I'd have been a better manager both in retail and at the ballet if I knew then what I know now in terms of my behaviour patterns and how best to communicate and work with others.

While I was at the ballet I went to my first personal development training. It was a course called *Money and You.* I thought it was about earning more money but it was all about me and my connection to money. I'd never been exposed to any type of personal work until then and I must admit I was challenged. I thought that even though there'd been some challenges in my life I had dealt with them OK. At this training I discovered this wasn't entirely the case.

This program was a rather heady fast-paced American-style *'Get in there, get your shit out and then move on'* type of training, with up-selling to other programs weaved into the mix. However, despite its slickness, this program did make me aware that I needed to work on myself personally. Through giving up my career as a flautist to my husband's business challenges I needed to find a happier me. I was relieved to be able to start letting go of my grief at surrendering a promising career and I began to realise that that grief is a necessary and important way of moving through emotional challenges.

Once I felt I'd dealt with that part of my life, there were many more areas that I wanted to look at and I became interested in mainstream psychology, particularly Jungian, as a means to explore my prolific dream life. When I think back on this start to my personal development I'm so grateful to the friend who suggested *Money and You*. It wasn't so much about the course but about being able to find a way to understand my own personal challenges and not bury them as I had been doing. In letting them see the light of day I could move on and not hide behind the successful career woman, who underneath doubted herself many times.

Professional development
- How often do I attend professional development programs?
- Am I inspired and challenged by these programs?
- Do I keep updating and adding new skills from personal development programs?

Combine personal and professional sections, rate from 1–10

Imagine finding smart new invigorating ways to make your career sing. What types of professional development topics would you love to explore and learn from? This is the ideal way to keep up-to-date with new research and learnings in your profession and I'm amazed at the large number of professional development programs on offer.

This is where I'd like to challenge you. Begin to make a list of the professional development programs that would inspire you, programs that would take you outside of the area you are working in now, yet intrigue and excite you. There's so much to be gained from putting yourself in an unfamiliar place to learn. It's like you're walking on the edge, immersing yourself in new ideas and inspirational teachings. You can take the themes, ideas, and suggestions back into your career and creatively invigorate yourself and your team.

One of my clients, a high-level executive assistant, moved from a corporate organisation to a university. She took all her corporate skills into a department where she was executive assistant to the dean. Part of her role was to proofread papers and she enjoyed this new role so much that she decided to enroll in a proofreading course. Proofreading has developed into a smart little business for her on the side – and a great way to create additional income with no expenses to set up shop. I know that in a few years' time she'll want to work part-time and here's a skill that can be leveraged into all forms of writing that requires editing.

I sometimes hear women say, *'If I had hired help at home, or more money I could have great quality of life.'* Let go of that statement. There will always be someone who seems more successful than you, financially or otherwise. It's important to give gratitude for the life you lead.

On that note, enjoy the knowledge from The Wheel. Keep working on it and in three months time, when you've worked through the rest of this book, go back, re-score the sections to reflect where you are now. I think you'll be pleasantly surprised.

Essentials of Creative Thinking

'Chaos is a normal part of any creative process. If it doesn't happen it usually means that nothing much is changing or being created and when this happens just go with it and let that critical voice take a backseat. Move ahead and let creativity into your life.'

When I worked at The Australian Ballet, people loved to come along and watch a working rehearsal (this was the final rehearsal before the dress rehearsal). Sponsors and their staff would attend and they were so popular that there was a ballot system for tickets. The rehearsal was in the theatre and would last an hour. Dancers were in costume or in leotards and tights.

The audience would see the onstage and backstage workings of a performance. There would be mechanists walking onto the stage, scenery being shifted around and lighting installed. The wardrobe staff would be adjusting costumes while the ballet artistic director was correcting moves and making new suggestions. The rehearsal would stop and start depending upon which areas required work.

This experience was exciting to the audience who rarely see a performance stripped back, or have the opportunity to watch part of the theatrical creation process. This is a great example of the creative process where a production is born out of many teams of people coming together to create magic. At the core there is a sense of passion and purpose as the production unfolds.

Creative thinking is like looking at your life through 3D glasses

Here's a terrific way to bring on creative thinking that works every time. All you have to do is look at your world through 3D glasses. Imagine for a moment you're watching a movie wearing 3D glasses. You're sitting back in the cinema relaxed and loving the movie. Now take the glasses off. What happens? Does the movie seem like it's lost some of its power? Before you took the glasses off you probably felt as if you were part of the story, drawn in, connected to the action and the plot. Now put the glasses back on. What is happening? Do you feel connected, absorbed and part of the show again?

It's the same when using creative thinking. Just think of something that you do every day, perhaps the journey to work. I'm sure that you know the route really well and maybe 'tune out' during this time. Now imagine taking another route or form of transport. What view of your city, town or countryside do you see now that you were previously unaware of?

A year ago, instead of taking a tram into the city of Melbourne, I went by train. The speed and the sights I had never seen before amazed me. The train travelled through suburbs I knew well but instead of driving past the facade of buildings, I saw the rear. I felt as if I was in a new city, and that was exciting. I saw a Melbourne I'd never noticed before with clever use of older buildings and well-designed additions. A bridge I used to jog under took on magnificent proportions when viewed from above. I noticed the Victorian design of the metal around the bridge, the shape of the arches and the aged beauty of this structure. I got off at Flinders Street Station feeling like a new woman. I was energised by this trip. I told my friends to travel by train instead of tram and see Melbourne through new eyes.

When we begin to ignite the creative woman inside ourselves, the 'magic' does happen. We find new energetic ways to live our life. We become confident in trusting and listening to the inner wisdom that sits within us. This wisdom can move our life or business out of stuck-ness and stagnation. We all have the ability to be creative. Creativity is not just the domain of artists.

I've worked with many women in law, medicine and accountancy who have embraced their creative self again. Although this creativity may have been hidden for many years, when these women put a vision board together they become artists. They don't hold back. In reality they've given themselves permission to be creative once more. Many female executives and business owners have loved playing music, dancing, singing and painting, etc. but have put these talents to one side as they developed their professional career.

As we move through this chapter, become aware of the past creative passions that you've forgotten. They have not disappeared. Give yourself permission to connect with those parts of your life. Keep remembering that you don't have to compete and be the standout person in creative thinking. At the end of this chapter are suggestions to help bring creativity back into your world.

Creative thinking begins at home

I suggest that you start in your home. Whether your home is one room or many, it's your special place and it's important that you have that place where you feel secure, safe and supported and that reflects everything about you. I can tell a great deal about a new person in my life when I visit their home. I love being in buildings that exude warmth and comfort with positive energy rather than walking into a perfectly decorated, cold sterile space.

Home is the place where we revive ourselves and recharge our batteries. These walls support us when we move into new and sometimes challenging times in our lives. I couldn't write this book from a space that wasn't my home. I love it. Whenever I walk in the door I feel happy and alive, even if I've had a tough day. It's like my home speaks to me, which is essential for inspiring my creativity.

Grow your creativity with friends who 'speak your language'

I suggest you hang out with people who have lots of energy

to keep the creative you growing. This is such a simple yet important ingredient to keep creativity in your life. I am strongly intuitive and need to have people around me who are genuine with deep, positive, caring energy rather than people who are dashing around madly trying to achieve more than others.

Start to seek out people who 'speak your language'. This means people who are truly interested in you, whether in your business or personal life. These women or men will have a passion and purpose in their life. I know that when I'm with friends who 'speak my language', we have inspiring fun together. In their company, time flies, I feel alive and new ideas come to me. I feel heard and listened to. Even if some of my creative ideas are over the top, these friends help me find new ways to leverage the ideas into my life or business.

I remember times when friends from my ballet days would stay with me over the Christmas holidays. We'd sit outside with a bottle of wine, laughing and talking about the special things in our lives and the challenges we were facing. Many times we didn't need to solve these problems, but just being in that supportive environment gave me a new creative vision with a 3D view of the challenge. My mood changed and I felt alive and energised knowing that whatever was happening to me was not as bad as I imagined. Eventually I knew there were ways to move through these challenges.

Imagine if every week we had a team of people who could sit down with us like this. We could all support each other, both in our achievements and our challenges. As part of this group we could all view the challenge through our own creative eyes. How would you feel? I know I would feel supported and invincible. My heart and soul would sing!

With this creative inspiration you could go back to your business with new energy. Imagine what you could achieve by having this support. This book is part of a plan to assist you in moving through the stop–start business challenges. Put on your 3D glasses, find new opportunities to grow and move through 'stuff'. At the core of all this is creative thinking.

How to use music in creative problem solving

On days when creative thinking seems to be a chore, use music to change your mood. Music has the power to change mindset. There is plenty of research from around the world that confirms this. Several years ago there was a whole issue of *Time Magazine* dedicated to the Science of Happiness. It included a poll asking, *'How happy are Americans?'* And when asked, *'What do you do to improve your mood?'* listening to music was the second highest. (First place was talking to family or friends.) Listening to music to improve mood was rated above meditating, taking a bath, exercising and socialising with friends.

- Play a piece of uplifting music for around 10 minutes (any longer and you will drift off with the music which is great but not part of this exercise).
- Use music that resonates within you.

- Sit in a quiet place where you won't be interrupted and put the challenge you have into one sentence.
- Let the music wash over and around you.
- When the music finishes write about the situation that was challenging you.
- Has it changed? What new thoughts, ideas or suggestions have arisen?
- Stay with this information and let it percolate for a few hours, maybe until the next day.
- Then look at the challenge using the insight and ideas that have come forward from the music. At first the ideas may seem quite odd and chaotic – this is part of the creative process.
- Refine the ideas into workable solutions.

This is a very brief introduction to music and creative thinking and as you move through the book there will be further and more in-depth creative problem-solving methods.

Using fun to think creatively

When we're in the process of creating new directions in our career and personal life, fun can be left behind. I know that I get caught up in finding ways to make all areas of my life work well and at times I forget about letting go and genuinely having fun. Fun is an important part of the creative process. It's important to keep an eye on growing and nurturing our business, however we can often forget to incorporate fun into the process.

Also, if a project gets stuck at some stage, pause and take time out to have fun: to just let go and laugh to get the energy back into the project. I often suggest to clients that they go off and see a comedy movie or read a light-hearted book. My escapism is to read chick lit and recently I got into erotic fiction. It's fabulous when I need to remove myself from the world. When I lost my dog Belita I spent the weekend mourning her, reading erotic fiction and drinking red wine. (I have to thank Belita for giving me permission to delve into this new exciting area of literature.) When I finished the books I was feeling a million dollars and enrolled in burlesque classes – and what a fun experience that was!

In a business environment I suggest to my clients that they use music to have fun. This time put on some fabulous upbeat music. Let the music move you. Dance as one of your favourite characters from a show or music video. Music is great for getting rid of inhibitions and opens up the creative spirit. At the end of these sessions it's important to harvest the energy. Use the fun session as a way to address and discover new ideas and ways to move through challenges.

I love this quote from Benjamin Zandler's book *The Art of Possibility*. He writes that Michaelangelo said, *'Every block of stone has a statue inside it and it is the task of the sculptor to discover it.'*

I believe that this can be true of all of us in this world. Until you go within and start creating another possibility, the person/block of marble stays the same but with creativity and vision, this piece of precious material can be transformed.

Exercises

1. Wish list

Put a wish list together of all that you want to do as a creative individual. Make the list as long as it can make be. Be mad, think creatively – it doesn't matter if some of the wishes are crazy: what you're doing is bringing back to life the creative inspiring woman.

For example:
- Laugh more
- Commit to learning constantly
- Travel constantly
- Buy standout heels
- Cook fabulous food
- Look after your body, go to the gym, get a trainer
- Have more candlelit baths
- Wear glamorous clothes
- Create a fabulous outdoor vegetable garden

(these are mine, what about you?)

2. Creative Diary

There are many ways that we can keep growing the creative parts of ourselves. These days you can even do this online using Pinterest, for example. With this pinboard-style photo-sharing platform you can create storyboards of your interests and hobbies. I've become a convert to

Pinterest as I find that there are so many inspirational pictures of my passions like food, clothes and travel. I feel alive and energised when I check out the range of posts on the site. I then add the images or videos onto my 'creative board' as I call it – a creative diary for the 21st Century!

Alternatively, you can buy a scrapbook and start writing and pasting articles and images that you connect with. You decide which modality works for you. Whether it's an online creative diary or scrapbook, both will keep the creative juices happening.

An Introduction to
Creative Visioning

Have you ever thought about how our world would be without visionaries – those people who had a dream and made it happen?

When we decide to live a life that makes our hearts sing, we must connect with our inner resources, those parts of ourselves that we may have put to one side as we pursued a career. I must add that you shouldn't regret the path you've been down. This path can create many opportunities to leverage your existing professional skills into a new vision.

When you move into this stage of life transition, it's important to develop a vision that excites. You've nothing to lose and everything to gain. I want to support you in taking the first step towards a more fulfilling life path, to move into this world of possibility. I know it's possible. I've followed my dreams and vision many times.

When we're able to put our dreams into an action plan, *that's* when the magic happens. For example, when I saw The Australian Ballet job advertised I remember thinking, *'This will be my dream job. How can I get it?'* It was as Manager of Corporate Development and at that time I was running a dance studio. I knew that I wanted to work for a company that would challenge me and give me the opportunity to grow my skills in performing arts business development. The ballet was the hook. I couldn't have worked for just any company – my passion was the performing arts and this was a dream job. I knew that I only had some of the qualifications: I had not raised money for arts organisations and I didn't have a large corporate network.

Yet I made it my mission to get this job. It was a passion for me, to imagine and visualise how my skills could translate into the job description. I knew that I loved connecting with organisations at a high level and that I was passionate about the arts. I had a business head too – my husband and I were turning tired apartments into stylish homes. After many interviews I got the job. I was ecstatic! It was like all the artistic and business parts of my life had come together. I could now use my expertise to grow corporate funding for the ballet.

When a dream job comes along and connects with our vision for this stage of life, it's like we have been connected to our life purpose – we feel alive in our body. Our whole being resonates. Life is perfect.

Remember, your life can take on this awakening once you decide to take a course of action towards a new path or vision that brings passion back into your life.

Visionaries

To assist you in moving forward I suggest that you become interested in people who follow their dreams in a grounded way. These people come from all areas of life and they have the courage to stand out from the crowd. Many of them can be role models as we move along a new path. It takes a strong inner spirit and desire to follow a path that doesn't have a road map.

As a food-lover I love reading stories of people who are now living a rural life. Most of them have left well-paid corporate careers and moved to rural areas to produce high-quality cheeses, heirloom vegetables, artisan breads and so on. They all have a connectedness, a passion for what they do. I must add here that the other essential ingredient is to be a bit crazy! These people have probably always had a secret passion to leave stability behind and found the courage to dive into a lifestyle that brings them great rewards and happiness.

How would it feel to be able to embrace that passionate part of yourself, put a vision together, follow it and have a life that is meaningful? How would it feel to have a life that leverages your present skills and translates them into a new purposeful business?

The basics of visioning

I find that it helps enormously to understand the framework for creating a vision and yet be able to let go of the part of our mind that wants explanations.

In the following chapters there's a four step visioning

program. I suggest music tracks that will help to open up your creative mind.

Each step will uncover a part of yourself:
Step 1 – Where are you now?
Step 2 – Create a perfect world.
Step 3 – What's stopping you?
Step 4 – Putting the vision together to create an action plan.

This creative process provides a new landscape – sort of like a tour guide introducing you to innovative pathways on your journey. You'll be encouraged to write about each of the steps, which will give you clarity. After writing at each step, you then assemble a collage. This represents the internal wisdom that is coming forward. Once it's out in the form of a collage you can connect with the new direction it's taking your life.

Visioning brings to the foreground images from the unconscious. Like seeds that grow into plants, these images have been sitting inside us and we often let them stay there. Until life changes that is, and then we need to find a new approach to bring them to life and create a life that is meaningful.

The seeds that create a vision are similar to bulbs put away in the dark each year, waiting to be brought out into the sunlight, to be planted and grow into beautiful fragrant flowers. Unless the seeds are brought out into the sunlight and planted, they can't grow. So it is with visioning.

If we keep our dreams and passions locked away in the dark, they don't see the light of day and have no way of putting down roots and growing. Visioning is about transforming ideas and concepts into a real-time possible product, life path or career direction.

Think like a visionary and embrace the chaos

'Visionary people face the same problems everyone else faces, but rather than get paralysed by their problems, visionaries immediately commit themselves to finding a solution.'

To take outmoded thinking and come up with innovative ideas and creative solutions, your inner wisdom must come into consciousness. Visioning paints pictures of solutions and brings forward images that help you to design methods of working and achieving remarkable goals and success. Often in the visioning process images can seem disconnected, however, from chaos comes stillness, creation and solutions.

It's much like a team of people brainstorming to find a solution to a situation. In this process people toss ideas into the circle, even if these ideas seem not to be connected. Yet in time some sort of order appears and the ideas eventually form a solution. Order eventually comes from chaos. Without chaos there would not be new ideas, creativity or ways of solving problems. Without chaos we wouldn't be human. It's critical to learn how to deal with, recover from and actually enjoy chaos.

'One must still have chaos in oneself to be able to give birth to a dancing star.'

FRIEDRICH NIETZSCHE

So here's your activity:

Think of 15 visionary people or products and how they've transformed our lives. Examples include: the internet, Richard Branson, credit cards, Oprah Winfrey.

I encourage you to start to think of this next stage of your life like a visionary. You may even like to put yourself in the shoes of one of these people and take on their persona for a few days. As you do this, imagine that you are an actor on the set of a movie. You're playing the character of one of these visionaries and the shoot of the movie takes six weeks. What you need to do is decide who you want to be, research the role, find out as much as you can about them.

Read about how this person transformed themselves into the visionary they became. What challenges and hurdles did they have to overcome? What were their dreams? How did they make their dream happen?

The next stage is production, so start to embody that person. How does it feel? I imagine that you find a new strength within and that nothing will stop you making this vision happen. You have supportive friends and family around you. Stay in character for as long as you can. (Actors often stay in character for the entire duration of the movie shoot.) The important part of this process is to connect with your inner visionary and, as you do this, to connect with the changes those visionaries made in their lives.

The power of music

I suggest that you use music that inspires you as you go through the following chapters. It will assist in creating a powerful vision.

Listening to music is the most powerful way for us to go into feelings – it has the potential to take us to so many different places. Music therapy is used in the care of the physically and emotionally handicapped, the aged, and in hospices for the dying. It's used in many medical interventions where Western drugs and scientific technology are gradually making way for ancient forms of healing from global cultures. For example, in old people's homes positive reactions have been noted when the elderly hear music from many decades ago. They become more animated, as if they come to life when surrounded by music that they recognise from their youth.

You can play music in your home and change your state of feeling at any time. Start thinking of ways that you can play pieces of music that are restful and tranquil at the end of the day. Sit down for a few minutes and let the music wash over you, taking away all that has happened that day.

Music takes you back in time. Think of (or even better listen to) the music from time gone by. Notice how you feel when you remember it. One of my great reminders is from when I was in the show *Jesus Christ Superstar*. Even though I was a flautist in the band for just 18 months, every time I hear the song '*I don't know how to love him*', I go back to the 70s, living with my boyfriend in Sydney.

The power of writing

Writing is another very powerful and important tool in this program: taking the language and visualisation from the music and giving it a written form. You need to do this to make the creation come into being. Writing a journal is incredibly powerful. When you have a problem or a difficult situation in your life, write for at least 10 minutes to gain clarity about what's happening and you'll find the situation doesn't appear so difficult. When you transpose your inner feelings and emotions onto paper they don't have a hold over you. This forms part of the foundations of this book and my coaching programs.

For example, when you think of a great dish of fabulous food, you write down the collection of ingredients that you'll need to bring this dish together. An architect who dreams up a building must design and write structural specifications first so that this dream can become a reality. Writing will help in this process of transformation. It's a way of bringing together an understanding of your creative inspiration or vision in each section of this program.

The power of collage

A picture tells a thousand words.

Collage is a visual representation of the visioning and writing process. By giving symbolic or pictorial form to this stage you have a visual representation to give you clarity. Your collage is the final presentation of all the stages of each part of this program and represents a combination of music, visioning and writing which come together in the creative experience. In architectural terms, you have constructed the building.

In the four steps of this program there will be four different collages, and at the end of the process these visual representations will amalgamate to form your unique structure or blueprint for the next stage of your life. Each image that you put onto paper will represent some aspects of your situation. Some pictures and what they represent will be clear, others may not.

The visual images are the *gold* and I want you to take a powerful position and stand behind your collages, like a miner, searching for the treasure hidden there. Your search will reveal riches from within. These deep hidden insights will keep building as you work through the program. It's the unconscious giving a conscious awareness of the great inner wisdom inside of yourself that all too often we don't pay attention to.

Your collage is like a storyboard, plan, or roadmap of how you can visualise your success. What you have is every step sitting in front of you. All you need to do is to follow this blueprint step by step for your success.

Step 1 of the Visioning Program: Where are you starting from?

This first stage of the creative visioning program is similar to pouring the foundation for a building, there must be a strong base to support the new home. Did you know that in Jungian psychology dreams featuring a home refer to our body? So the metaphor of a home (a new home) is an ideal way to begin transforming your life.

Now that you've read through the previous chapters, I imagine you have enormous insight into 'what makes you who you are'. I hope that in writing your story, and finding the creative 'you' there is now a woman wanting to move into the passionate life that is possible.

I had a client who went through major career change. She had the courage to leave a high-level executive job that was exhausting and demanding and her goal was to create a new career path within three months. She did it and I was amazed at the way that she embraced the creative coaching and visioning program. As a result of working through the collages, she was determined to find a career where she was valued and inspired.

This client was a creative and inspiring woman, and within the three-month period she found a job at a university. I remember she said to me, '*I now have a life I love! I enjoy working with the team around me; my boss appreciates me and my working hours are reduced. Sure I earn a little less but I'm truly happy.*'

My client went through the coaching detailed in each of the chapters you have read and are about to read. She discovered her passions and what she was missing out on; she found out about the real and purposeful parts of herself; let go of the stress and exhaustion too. I noticed a change in the way she spoke, there was more excitement in her voice. She's now living a life she wants and feels fulfilled everyday.

When she reached this stage, to celebrate her success, she took off on an overseas trip to Italy. I remember she had told me about this opportunity to go away with friends. It was tempting yet she felt that she should use the money to pay off some of her mortgage. I said to her that obviously it was her decision, but asked her, '*What inspires you? How can you reward yourself for all this personal work?*' She decided to go on the trip and came to see me when she returned. Here was a woman with an Italian spring to her step, radiant, alive and happy. She told me it was one of the best holidays she had ever been on.

This is a terrific example of the power of the creative visioning process from the first foundation through to the final stage. You move your life along, transform, change, invigorate because you can. You do not leave anything out.

The tools for each step are as follows:
- Visioning with music for approximately five minutes
- Writing about the visioning
- Collage

Step 1 is the time to reveal all the tough bits, challenges, frustrations and your life path so far.

Vision Script

You may like to record each of the four visioning scripts so that you can hear your voice guiding you. Remember to read the words slowly as this helps the relaxation process. Play the recording back to make sure you're not speaking too quickly, (a good tip is to breathe deeply between each sentence). If you're unable to record your voice I suggest that you quietly read the script to yourself as you move through the start of each section.

Music

What you need to assemble for this stage is a piece of music that inspires you. I suggest classical music as it has a regular beat and the style of music will move deep within you. As you will have read in the previous chapter, music is the core to opening us up to our deep internal resources. Don't worry if you're unable to find the classical tracks I recommend. Put on music that speaks to you though it must not have vocals.

Suggested music selections

Mozart, Overtures, Neville Mariner Academy of St Martin in-the-Fields

Mozart, *Sinfonia Concertante K.364, Concertante K190* Israel Philharmonic

Brahms, *String Sextet no.1 in B Flat. Op.18/No 2 in G. Op. 36*, Berlin Philharmonic Octet

Schubert, *String Quartet in C Major D 956*, Amadeus Quartet

Anton Bruckner, *Symphony no. 4* ("Romantic"), Herbert von Karajan, Berlin Philharmonic

Respighi, *Pines of Rome*, Louis Lane, Atlanta Symphony Orchestra

Brahms, *Violin Concerto in D major, Double Concerto A minor*, Royal Concertgebouw

"Brazil" Compilation, Universal Recording

Barrio Latino Paris, by Carlos Campos, George V Records

Time and Space

Find a quiet space within your home away from family and pets. You can either move through the four steps one after the other (this will take about two hours), or you can move through each step separately (this will take about 30 minutes). If you decide to move through each step of the visioning separately, try not to leave too many days in between. I suggest a week as maximum. The reason is that one stage builds upon the other and it would be a little like watching a movie over four separate screenings. Each time you watch the movie you'll have a little bit of catching up to do to remember what happened in the previous section.

Writing

This is the time to buy a beautiful journal to write about each of the visioning steps. By keeping a journal you'll have a meaningful record of how you moved your life along through this program.

My choreographer friends tell me that when they've completed a piece of their work they like to remind themselves how they began the creative process. By the time they finish the work they have a stage production that's a living, breathing testament to their creative skills. It's as if they produced a new life. They've given birth to a new production that several months ago was a creative concept in a notebook. It's the same with this visioning process.

Collage

A collage is a visual representation of the vision or landscape and now you know that this is your inner wisdom coming to the surface – and all the creative inspirational parts of you that have been hidden for many years.

For the collage you'll need the following:
- Poster-size paper
  I suggest you get several poster-size pieces of paper in colours that speak to you.

- Magazines

  Collect as many magazines as you can. It doesn't matter what type they are. Just let your unconscious mind choose them. If you don't have any lying around the house I suggest you go to a charity shop where there are usually lots to choose from.
- Glue

  A glue stick is all that's required.

Now you are ready to begin the visioning program.

Step 1: Where are you at this stage of your life?

Look at where you are now. Think of yourself as the star of this next stage of your life. You are setting down the foundations necessary to create and turn around your life.

Gather your journal, magazines, paper and glue together before you commence the visioning. It's important to keep the process and energy going from the music and visioning script until you have finished the collage.

Visioning

I suggest you play a calming piece of classical music for this stage such as the first movement of Mozart, *Sinfonia Concertante*.

Relaxation script

Take time to become comfortable, whether you are on a chair, on the ground, wherever you are, just slowly let yourself relax. And as you relax, let your body sink into the surface that is supporting you, wherever you are ... Know that by letting yourself relax even more you are going to be able to move deeply into this visioning exercise ... Be aware of your breath as it moves through your body, paying attention to the rise and fall of your chest ... Also let your breath move through every part of your body, flowing into the sore parts of your body, bringing nourishing healing to those parts of you ... Letting every cell of your body be nourished by this cleansing breath.

Visioning slow down

As you relax into this place within yourself, let the music flow around and within you ... Just let the music take you into this visioning that will reveal so much. This is the foundation of the program ... Just be aware of what it is that has brought you here, where you are in your life or your business. And what is it that you want to get from this visioning ... You are starting at the beginning and this is where you need to vision exactly where you are right now. This place will form the foundation of all the visioning experiences ... And even if you do not see pictures, which can be quite common, just use your imagination and this will guide you in this visioning exercise ... The experience will still be powerful for you. So imagine that you are an artist with a blank canvas. I want you to go into the situation that you want to change or where you need more clarity ... What do you see? Are there people around, sounds, smells, where are you, outside or inside? Create this picture or painting in front of you. And just start to explore and go within. How do you feel? What is happening? Become inquisitive. Do not move away, just stay in this place. Really embody this situation that you want to change … How is the picture looking? Are there colours, people, places that stand out? Start to fill out this painting of the situation, and make it come to life inside of yourself … And as you do that begin to notice what is happening to your body. What is arising from your sensations, feelings, emotions, and thoughts, what is happening? Even if all of this is new to you, do not discount what is happening. Just be aware that this internal vision and wisdom is coming forward in ways that you may not have experienced. This is important information.

End of visioning
Taking as much time as you need, slowly start to bring your attention back into the room … Slowly and steadily come back to this room.

Writing
Start to write for a few minutes about what vision or experience you had. Don't censor your writing. If you can only write a few sentences that's absolutely fine. Write for no longer than five minutes.

Collage

Now tear out images from the magazines. Do not censor – just tear without thinking. Imagine that you're a child again. You're letting yourself make as much mess as you want. This creative work is fun! It doesn't matter if you've no idea why you chose these images or words, just tear them. Take about five minutes to assemble the material for your vision, and then put them together onto the vision board. Remember the child in you again. Just stick them down in a way that feels right for you. Take another five minutes to complete this part.

Now you have finished Step 1:

- Ask yourself, *'How do I feel looking at this creation, my collage?'*
- Move through the images and words on the collage and ask yourself, *'How do they connect to this stage of my life?'*
- The collage may be self explanatory regarding your life at present, or there may be images on the collage that you do not understand.
- If there are images unknown to you, ask yourself, *'How could these connect to my life at present?'*
- What you're doing is starting the transformative experience. The images that are unknown may become clearer over the next day.

You are ready now to move onto Step 2 of the creative visioning program.

Step 2 of the Visioning Program: Create a perfect world

Now that you have clarity from Step 1 and you're able to articulate and picture your life at present, it's time to take a gigantic step and move into discovering the passionate upbeat woman you are. In Step 2 the question I will ask you for the visioning is, *'It's a perfect world, how can you achieve whatever you need?'*

I like to use the metaphor of 'opening the curtain on your show'. What is this step going to reveal? What do you and the audience see when the curtain goes up? Is the scenery lavish and are the costumes grand? Or is the set minimalistic with simple but beautiful costumes reflecting the woman you are? Step 2 contains all your past achievements, talents, longings and more. This is where you get to be the director of your show for the next stage of your life.

I can remember the feeling from many years ago when I joined the band of *Jesus Christ Superstar*. I was 21 and it was my first professional job. I'd trained all my life for this and I had goosebumps as the band started playing the overture. It was as if all my dreams, passions, desires, loves and more had come together. I was in heaven. I could have played that musical score for hours. I was in a new world that I had dreamt about since childhood.

For the 18 months I was in that show, my inner deep connection with the music never wavered, (which is unusual when performing eight shows a week). Whenever I hear the music from *Jesus Christ Superstar* my body immediately goes back to the show: the theatre; my friends; the orchestra pit; the people around me; my boyfriends and especially my VW Beetle which the props guys had painted with a big *JCS* logo on the side.

I find that with this step my clients remark that the vision often contains parts of their life they had forgotten, especially their achievements and the dreams that were overlooked as they followed a career path. Now is the time to let it all out. This is your life and more revealed.

Step 2 is the time to ask the question *'Where can I take myself and my business in a perfect world?'* Get ready for the big reveal!

Visioning

Put on another piece of music. Perhaps the Brahms Violin and Cello Concerto, 3rd Movement.

Relaxation script

Relax, once again going into your body and letting yourself relax internally, and be as comfortable as you can be, wherever you are seated … And as you relax let your body sink into the place that is supporting it … Know that letting yourself relax even more you will be able to sink into this experience … Be aware of your breath as it moves through your body … be aware of the rise and fall of your chest … And also let your breath move into the sore or tight parts of your body, letting those parts relax even further … Let every cell of your body be nourished by this cleansing breath moving through you … And be aware of the sounds around you and know that they are part of the experience, and be with this without judgment … Just keep relaxing into this experience.

Visioning

I want you to go within your body and begin to see another picture or vision in front of you, showing you what this situation or stage of your life is like when there is a solution … Let your imagination run wild … What you are doing is opening the door to the riches and solutions to this situation that is within you … Where are you in this experience? Who is around you? Where are you? Once again you can imagine that you are an artist in front of a canvas, what are you painting? Where are you, are you outside, inside, are there people around you? Is it warm, cold, what are you wearing? Just keep filling out this picture … What does it feel like to have this situation solved? In this inner world you are able to achieve whatever you need to achieve for success in your life, just let these wonderful images and solutions appear in front of you … This is a perfect world and you can make whatever you desire happen … Are there other images coming forward that can help you with completing this picture? Remember that whatever is coming forward is from your own internal wisdom and that you are capable of bringing this to completion … Even though you may not be clear about the images, words, pictures or whatever is happening, stay with this information. You will be able to move through this situation to a conclusion … This is the start of moving towards a successful result … This is a creative process and will take the time that it needs for you to assemble all your inner and outer tools to bring clarity to the plan or road map you need to embark upon to bring conscious life to this new creation and the next stage of your life.

End of visioning

Take as much time as you need to bring your attention back to the room … Slowly and steadily come back into the room, stretching your body, and then slowly opening your eyes … And then take a few minutes to write about this experience of visioning for success – a perfect world.

Writing

Write for a few minutes regarding this section of the visioning. Remember not to censor, just let your pen keep the story from the vision alive. Write for no longer than five minutes.

Collage

Repeat the collage making process from Step 1. This time I'm sure that the process will be faster. Remember to give yourself five minutes to tear out images and words that relate to the vision; and then five minutes to stick them on the poster-size paper.

I suggest that you then spend a further 10–15 minutes connecting with the collage. The images, pictures and words will reveal the next stage of your life. You have a storyboard sitting in front of you. Here are some questions to help you understand this collage:

- Which image stands out to you?
- What significance does it have in your life, past, present or for the future?
- Now look at other significant images. What do they mean to you?
- If there are words what is their significance?
- Images that appear unclear will become clearer over the next days and weeks. Keep going back to them.
- How does the collage connect to your journal writing?
- Does the collage now provide more information about this next stage of your life?

As you move through each step of the visioning and collage sections, I suggest that you sit the collages in a place that can be easily seen. They will serve as a constant reminder of your inner passion and potential. You have embarked on this journey, and the vision, writing and collage are now giving you a roadmap forward.

You may find that new energy and enthusiasm is arising in your body as stuck energy regarding challenges is moved and the creative inspiring part of you takes over. You have always had inner resources and imagination. The magical part is now – when you let yourself connect with the passionate woman you are.

I name this stage of the process 'A solution appears'. You are discovering new solutions to unstick your problem. You're seeing it with new eyes. You have added knowledge from your inner self. Your show has a form and your audience can see what sort of show you're about to put on. This show is uniquely yours and no one else will be producing a spectacle the way you do. This is an important point. Your collage reflects the unique passionate person you are – and the next few steps put together details and an action plan to ensure your show opens to a full house.

Step 3 of the Visioning Program: What's stopping me?

So now you're half way through the journey of directing your own production – the new stage of your life direction – and this part is the *gold*. I'm going to ask you to bring the critical part of you into the visioning – the part that can sabotage and challenge.

I'm sure you'll know this inner critic. She sits within you and stops you from following new opportunities. This part belongs to the 'young woman' in you and she may confront you with questions like, '*Who do you think you are?*' and, '*Why do you want to do this?*'

This visioning exercise brings you face to face with the critical parts of yourself. And when you become aware of the role they have in your life you can do something to lessen their hold over you. These critical voices were formed many years ago to protect you, however, you do not need them to have control over you now. They are called Protector Controller and we all have them in varying forms. Quite often they sit on your shoulder and keep up a steady dialogue to stop you in your tracks.

This section speaks loudly to me. I've had to overcome a flood of critical voices that could have stopped me even moving into my career in music. I can remember when I decided to leave New Zealand as a 19-year-old flautist, and move to Adelaide to study. I knew no one apart from the name of the flute teacher, David Cubbin, who fortunately accepted me as a student.

In those days it was bold and yet I knew that to grow my career as a flautist I had to get out of New Zealand. For many months I felt sick in the stomach and had people around me questioning me with, *'Do you really think you'll make it as a flautist in Australia? You'll be all on your own…'* My parents told me they couldn't support me financially and so I had to take the risk and find part-time work as soon as I got there. There were many times when I could have retreated and stayed safe in New Zealand, but my heart told me that if I didn't make the trip, I would live an unfulfilled life. I knew this to be true and yet felt so alone.

Now I understand that the Protector Controller part of me was loving this challenge. She wanted to keep me safe and under her control. I knew it would be easier to lead a mediocre life. I didn't know what to do and felt anxious and depressed at the thought of being somewhere new on my own and starting a new life. And yet despite these feelings, my heart kept telling me not to listen to these friends, family and my own inner critic – it told me to get on the plane and go!

Over 40 years later I'm so relieved that I had the

courage to move to Australia. I hate to think what could have happened to my life if I didn't follow my dream and my heart. And still I remember the first months in Adelaide, being homesick and alone with my inner critic having a great time. I hid the fear that was inside myself for some time and it was only when I began to excel as a flautist did I realise that, 'yes', I had made the right decision. It was tough, but to stay behind would have been worse.

This story demonstrates the power of the inner critic that we all have inside ourselves. We have grown up with this negative voice and the challenge and the *gold* is to *slay the dragon* and move ahead. It really is like a mythological battle – to move into new life you have to confront your enemies. I thank the challenging years of psychotherapy training in helping me understand this part of myself and what a hold our critical mind can play when we don't understand or confront it. Many dreams suffer this way.

So I would love you to move into Step 3 knowing that you will come out alive and feeling a lot lighter; that once you're able to name the critical parts of yourself there is a glorious sense of saying, *'You're not going to have a strong hold over me ever again!'* This understanding is like going on a diet and losing a heap of weight. You feel refreshed, rejuvenated and ready for a new look at life.

Step 3 is the time to ask the question, *'What's holding me back from achieving this outcome?'*

Visioning

For music I suggest a slow movement from one of the Brahms String Sextets.

Relaxation script

Once again going into your body … Just knowing that the music will take you again back into a deep place within … Just go within your body and let yourself relax into the surface that is supporting you … And as you relax even more know that you will be able to sink even more deeply into this relaxation and visioning exercise … Be aware of your breath as it moves through your body, the rise and fall of your chest as your breath moves into all the tight or sore places in your body. Let those parts relax even further … Let all the cells of your body be nourished by this breath … And all you need to do is just keep relaxing into this place within …

Visioning

This place can reveal to you insight and information on whatever is holding you back from resolving or gaining clarity about this stage of your life… Whether this is personal or professional… And once again become a painter with a blank easel in front of you or whatever way you want to imagine or visualise this stage… And let the music go further within helping you understand how you can become familiar with the parts of you that are stopping you from creating and having success in your life … And a solution to this situation … Are there new skills that you need to learn? Or can you use what you already know? Are there old patterns or awareness's that keep coming in? And are you familiar with whatever may be stopping you from reaching your potential? Now is the time to really get to know those parts of yourself and bring them forth into consciousness so they do not continue to have a hold over you … Just let whatever needs to come up for you, symbols, pictures, feelings, emotions, awareness. Whatever there is to give you more clarity about these parts that have prevented you from moving forward.

End of visioning

As this visioning comes to an end let yourself take as much time as you need to bring your attention back into the room… Let yourself slowly return to consciousness, maybe stretching, moving your body and then slowly open your eyes … And begin to write for a few minutes about this visualisation of, *'What's stopping you from achieving success in your life?'*

Writing

Write for a few minutes regarding this section of the visioning. Remember not to censor, just let your pen keep the story from the vision alive. Write for no longer than five minutes.

Collage

Repeat the collage making process from Step 1 and 2. This time the process will be even faster. Remember to give yourself five minutes to tear out images and words that relate to the vision; and then five minutes to stick them on the poster size paper.

The *gold* of creative success is in this section – becoming acquainted with the obstacles that stop us, whether it's parents or well-meaning friends telling us, *'You won't earn much money with this idea.'*

This is where you realise that many of the negative behaviours and situations in your life are starting to lose their grip on you because now you're consciously aware of how and why you've reacted to these situations in a negative way. These behaviours have been like a vine that's been climbing over a house, obscuring windows and the many beautiful features of this building. Now the vine is falling away to reveal a building that is unique in character and design – You!

Step 4 of the Visioning Program: Moving forward

Now that you've got to the final part of the four step visioning plan, I imagine that you've been surprised by the creative woman that you are. I know that many of my executive clients tell me they aren't creative at the start of visioning and guess what happens? It's like they have permission to let out the inner artist, femme fatale or whatever you may want to call her. We all have these rather lovely parts that make up ourselves.

I know that when I let go or give permission to the rather rigid old-style headmistress in me, a new energised woman emerges. She is funny, sensual, finds life flows and doesn't worry too much about having to conform. I know that I need to keep moving through regular check-ins with my visioning self, to let myself grow and have confidence to be the woman that I love.

I'm never wrong about women who do this program. Each of them has a story that is intriguing and powerful; a story that was swept under the carpet through work challenges; a story that has to be told. We all underestimate our life stories but without remembering our past we would not be who we are today – we must remember both the challenges and the achievements.

My experience of the 4 Steps of Visioning

All stages of the visioning program mirrors the path I took several years ago in putting my business *Corporate Creative Directions* into a form. I had a dream that I could incorporate creative thinking into executive coaching, yet I had to find a way to be able to put all the parts of the program and methodology together.

My Step 1 was starting with the dream: I had an idea and I had knowledge. But being a creative I didn't know how to articulate *Corporate Creative Directions'* program. I could see it, hear it and yet to put this into a written version was scary – a bit like having pieces of a jigsaw puzzle scattered randomly all over a table.

My Step 2 filled out the picture for me: in my collage I had assembled beautiful objects, great food, wine, architecture and more. I felt alive and inspired. I created a collage that took my inner passion to an external form. I saw that the work I would create was going to ignite me firstly, and create new life for me and for my clients. There was a feeling of excitement, and yet also the concern about how to get this new creative coaching method out there.

So, in Step 3 I had to confront my enormous group of inner critics. I have many and though I may appear confident, successful and together (and I am most of the time!), when that inner critic hits I have to work hard to keep him away from me. There are times when I hear that part questioning my life path now, suggesting that my world would be a lot easier if I'd just stuck to psychotherapy and become a therapist. Yes it would have been easier, but it didn't excite me.

This section is the turning point as you work through your career challenges. It's also, as I have mentioned, the *gold*. This is where you realise that negative thought patterns have a hold over you and that they must be brought into conscious awareness; to be exposed to the light of day and laid right in front of you. Do not let them sabotage your life again.

In Step 4 my vision came into reality in a way that I found quite goosebumpy! At this time, I was feeling ready to get my new business up and running, yet I still had to put a methodology and structure to the program – and for me this was a problem. Then one day I went along to a businesswomen's lunch in Byron Bay and won a one-hour session with a copywriter. A few days later I rang Luella and arranged a meeting at my home.

When Lue arrived we both looked at each other in shock, as if we were old friends. I had never met Lue yet still remember connecting with her immediately on the doorstep of my home. And this is how Step 4 happened for me: it was getting the vision out into an action plan; packaging all the creative ideas, thoughts, knowledge and music into a form. *'From chaos comes structure'*. From the visioning comes form. And it's exactly like putting the pieces of a jigsaw puzzle together.

Lue and I worked together for many weeks refining the CCD offering, particularly the visioning method you are working through now. Translating high-performance techniques from the sporting world and performing arts into wording people could understand was both a challenging and a liberating process.

And this is the importance of Step 4: it's a coming together of all your visioning, writing and collages into the finale. This almost exactly mimics the creative process that a choreographer or composer goes through to deliver their work to an audience. You are now entering the finale of your show.

Step 4 brings together all the previous stages. The collage will reveal a visual picture that contains the next stage of your life or career path. It's like putting the last pieces of your jigsaw puzzle together – the finished piece showing your path forward. What you'll create in the next chapter is an action plan with steps to move you into this picture over an established time frame.

Stage 4 is the time to see the unfolding of the next stage of your life.

Visioning
Music suggestion is the Mozart, Overture, *The Marriage of Figaro.*

Relaxation script
Once again going into your body … Let yourself relax

into the chair or surface that is supporting you ... knowing that the music will take you again to a deep place inside ... a place full of riches ... And as you relax even more into this place, become aware of your breath ... as it moves through your body ... the rise and fall of your chest as your breath moves into all the sore and tight places inside of yourself ... nourishing every cell internally ... And all you have to do is to keep relaxing into this experience within ... that's right.

Visioning

Now you have so much inside information on the path to success in your personal and professional life. I want you to let the music take you towards a plan, a blueprint. This is what you will take away with you to start this new stage of your life ... Now bring together all the visioning, writing and the collages that you have created. And start to form a plan or a blueprint ... You can also become an artist again, standing in front of your canvas, what are you going to paint now? Remember that this is the start of an exciting way of you definitely changing the situation you came here with ... To now create success and creative knowing about this next stage of your life whether it be personal or professional. You have all the information and inner wisdom now sitting outside of yourself ready to take form. Start to open up this new stage and further potential to your life ... So what is the picture you are painting or what is happening to you now that gives you insight into your success? Where are you, who is around you, fill out the picture, what are the sounds … smells … are you outside, inside, in which part of the world are you? What are you wearing and what are you doing? You can combine all your business and personal expertise with this creative unfolding and insight … You may want, with the help of the music, to put these plans into a structure with goals for you to attain over a certain period of time … And you may want to keep regularly reviewing this understanding and refining whatever you need to do to attain your creative potential and success. So now in this final visioning bring all these wonderful and amazing insights into reality … Remember that whatever has come forth is totally possible as these insights have come from within you. And that from this place, you are the master of your own destiny… So let yourself relax into this new exciting stage of your life.

End of visioning
So now that the music is drawing to a close start to bring your attention slowly back into the room taking as much time as you need to become fully present … Slowly moving your body, taking all the time you need to come back … and then start writing about this final experience of, *'The blueprint for the creative success of your personal and professional life.'*

Writing
Once again write about the insights and images that have come up from the visioning. You may want to write more

in this section. What will happen is your inner world of visioning is bringing into focus a picture showing you how to move through the next stage of your life. Imagine you've been walking along one of the beautiful Cinque Terre tracks. You have several kilometres to go until the next town. You can see it in the distance. And as you keep walking, the village comes into focus. You can see your destination more clearly now.

Collage

Repeat the five minute tearing and five minute pasting process.

So you've arrived at your destination. As you've moved through the four steps each one has built upon itself. And with a starting point that might have been, *'I need to change my life,'* you now have opened up to new insight both in your career and personal life.

Congratulations!

This is the final act and it's important to make it memorable. Take time to immerse yourself in the images that you've put together into the collage. Ask yourself where they fit in your life. *Do you connect to some past areas of your life?* It could be in areas where you may have wanted to take your career but instead opted for a safe path at the time.

Spend a bit more time absorbing this final collage – at least 20 minutes taking in the images and words. See where you've placed the images and importantly, ask yourself, *'How does the collage feel to me?'* You may want to write more about this journey and that's the reason for a journal. It is your personal story and will remind you where you came from and where you are now. Remember the story about how a choreographer or composer works? A composer begins with a blank sheet of paper and then fills in the melody, harmony, structure and instrumentation of a piece of music. It's the same for you: you started with the basics of where you are now in your life, no frills, and now look – you have moved to a finished composition!

Have courage. If the final collage is telling you to follow a path that you've resisted, now is the time to say *'Yes!'*

I have a friend from my ballet days who is now working in New York. Tim had always wanted to live in New York so he decided to apply for a Green Card. This was a time consuming process that required him to fill out endless paperwork and move through a lengthy bureaucratic process. After several years he was issued with a Green Card and moved to an exciting city not knowing how he would support himself. What courage! He got a job in a Broadway musical and, to supplement his income, had to work in menial jobs that many in the performing arts know well. He kept searching for opportunities and he's now been in New York for over seven years.

I admire him. He had a dream and he made that dream happen. It was not easy, yet I look at his journey and see Tim as an inspiration. He didn't give up when there were tough times: he immersed himself in his dream. This example shows how important it is for us to follow our passions and find a way to live a life that uplifts us.

This step of the visioning will bring the four visioning stages together. Your path will come into focus. The show that you are producing has now become a form. So well done! You have taken action and put your production together.

When we get to this stage regarding opportunities for a new or more inspired life path, there is a great sense of elation and relief. Deep down you've always been aware of the smart passionate person you are, it's just that life and other challenges got in the way.

Now that you've completed the final collage, ask yourself, 'What's the first thing that I'm going to do to start moving the next stage of my life forward?' Just let your inner self tell you. There will be something in the final collage that jumps out at you – embrace this knowing. Connect with the photograph, illustration or words. Ask yourself, 'What does this part of the vision board mean to me now?'

In the next chapter there'll be a series of questions to develop the four steps into an action plan with time frame and goals to ensure your production hits the stage or screen.

Stay and luxuriate in the images that stand out to you. I find the images that jump out at me remind me of parts of my life that I have swept under the carpet and, to be honest, challenge me. I connect to the images, feel alive and know at this point there is no turning back if I am going to be true to myself. This collage is talking to you so be truthful to yourself. Does the vision board send you suggestions to move along a new path both personally and professionally? Take that trip overseas to a part of the world you had always wanted to visit? Get fit, move house, buy a new car? Take some time out of your life to rest and rejuvenate?

After my husband's death I had a dream that showed me very clearly that I needed to trust and take time out to rest. I still remember this dream. I am driving along Highway One, Big Sur, California in a convertible car. As the car goes around a bend, I fly out of the car into the ocean below. I'm afraid that the water will be so deep that I won't be able to swim to the surface. But I'm surprised to find the water is only waist deep and I can simply stand up. The relief is enormous.

This dream gave me the courage to shift to Byron Bay for a few years. I told myself that I must follow my heart – just as I advise my clients to. I moved to Byron not knowing a single person and immediately felt supported by the energetic healing environment of this special part of Australia.

Now is the time for you to immerse yourself in the creative collage that you've produced. Go out and get it laminated so that you have a permanent reminder of this stage of your life. And in the next chapter there will be an action plan to assist in bringing your production onto the stage.

Celebration

This is a diversion before you embark on the action plan and it's an important part of the visioning steps. Most of us are not great at acknowledging our wins so this is about spending some time celebrating and acknowledging the place that you've come to.

How about getting out the sassy vibrant woman that sits inside of you? How does it make you feel to hear these words? Do you laugh, giggle or dismiss her? Get her into action in whichever way works for you and ask yourself, *'What have I always wanted to do to embrace the feminine soul that sits inside of me?'* As businesswomen it's easy to let that part go especially as we move further up the corporate ladder.

This stage is about giving yourself permission to celebrate with friends and family in a way that makes you feel proud of what you have achieved in the past and at present. I'm only too aware that we live in a world that forgets about celebrating wins and how this can stem from family and educational backgrounds. 'Tall Poppy Syndrome' is a well-documented social phenomenon in

Australian culture that describes our criticism of those who stand out too much.

When I joined the ballet I became part of an organisation that celebrated achievements such as birthdays, promotions, productions, and many more events. In this environment I felt supported and acknowledged in all that I did and this was important. I come from a family of five kids where we had to work hard for whatever was wanted in life, yet there was very little time to feel that hard work was acknowledged. The message was, *'You're one of five, so don't expect any special treatment.'* I imagine that for some readers these words will resonate.

I've often admired Italian and Greek families who celebrate birthdays, religious events, achievements and more. I'm quite envious of the supportive family group my Italian neighbour has around him. For example, recently he went to see his nephew swim in a national race here in Melbourne and he said that the whole family turned up to see this 10-year-old swim. I can only imagine how this young boy's confidence was boosted by the loving support around him.

Many of my executive clients and high-level musicians tell me that they feel embarrassed when their achievements are recognised, whether in a newsletter or at a celebratory event. Is this an Australian/New Zealand phenomenon? Now that you've come through the challenges that you faced at the start of the book, how do you feel about having a celebration?

Hopefully you'll have come back in touch with the

real 'You', the woman who's successful, smart and well educated. And hopefully you've also found the part of you that has a plan to create greater potential and happiness in her life.

So as you near the end of the book, kick off your heels; sit back with friends; have a few wines and let go of the expectations you continuously put on yourself to achieve. What has this expectation done to your personal and professional life? Are you now able to give yourself permission to enjoy the large and small achievements with honesty, considering where you've come from?

I looked forward to sponsor nights at the ballet. The dancers would attend the cocktail parties I organised to meet the corporate sponsors of the production. These events were quite often full of French champagne, quality wines and stimulating company. When the sponsors left I would kick off my high heels and together with the dancers we'd sit back, have a few more wines and relax at the end of a long night. This was a terrific way for the dancers and I to get to know each other too.

I loved those nights and they reminded me of my days as a flautist. There was nothing better than having a glass of wine at the bar at the Opera House, looking out through the Green Room windows to Sydney Harbour all lit up with lights twinkling from the apartment blocks lining the shores. I'd go home tired and happy after nights that were fulfilling in so many ways.

When you get into the habit of celebrating your success with friends and workmates you feel supported.

There is a sense of standing tall with your achievements and work place challenges don't seem to have a hold over you. I know this area well and remind myself to celebrate my wins; to go out and have a massage or facial; buy that bag or those shoes I've had my eye on.

In the next chapter there's an action plan to follow that leads your vision towards a results-based finale, whether it's developing your career where you work or leveraging your expertise into exciting new career directions.

Action Plan

Now that you've reached the finale of the 4 Step visioning program this is the time to begin connecting deeply with the vision board and writing. There'll be an enormous amount of information sitting in the collages. Some of the visuals and words will jump out at you and these are the areas to concentrate on first.

Think of this part of the book as the action plan to create a life and career that sings to you. This is where your production 'hits the road or stage'; it's where your heart beats strongly and there's no more pretending or denying the path that you're on. In the visioning your unconscious has reminded you of past achievements, passions, dreams, desires and all the areas of your life that you need to engage with. You must not leave them as 'maybes' for when you have more time, or more finances. Do not procrastinate. Move forward. The right time is now.

On this journey you've put together a jigsaw puzzle that gives you a picture of your path – even if not all of it makes sense to you straight away. For example, when I started on my psychotherapy journey I spent time in the USA and was exposed to some of the world's leading teachers of meditation, ecstatic movement, body-centred and Jungian psychology. I didn't know exactly what I'd do with all these skills but several years later the exploration came together into *Corporate Creative Directions*.

One of my coaching clients had become stale and tired in her career and wanted to seek out a director level role. She had a second wind after finishing the visioning steps, went out and bought herself a whole new wardrobe to represent the high-level corporate woman she was. It took her six months from the end of the visioning program to find a job that was challenging and fulfilling enough for her. She said that the program had taken her out of the stuck-ness of both her personal and professional life.

I remember when she told me about the interview for this job, she said she'd felt too laid back as she hadn't been feeling well. As a result she imagined she may not be considered. My client was wrong. She got the job and I explained that after working through the visioning she was happier within herself and now realised that she had enormous expertise in the career path she was following.

Through the 4 Step program she had created a vision board showing her the next stage of her career and life pathway. Importantly there was a passion and feeling of aliveness within my client unlike when we had first met to talk about coaching. Then I saw a woman with impressive credentials appear defeated and resentful of the daily challenges she faced. Six months later the new happier her had come through in the interview. She had the necessary qualifications for the role and what she needed to do was to deeply believe in herself and bring this knowing into the room; knowing too, that if this wasn't the job for her there would be another.

Developing your story

So now what is needed is to develop the story within you from the visioning stages. Keep refining the writing from the collage into 'your story' – it can be a very short story or as long as a novel. What you're doing is cementing the next stage of your life within you. You have to connect with it. Live it, see it and believe that you can move ahead into a new stage of your professional and personal life.

Here's a set of questions that you can work on to help move ahead. They cover every part of the visioning process and will become a workable framework for your life. This is your story – no one elses. Your production is now going through the final logistics stage to make sure it works in the theatre.

Write the answers in your journal and spend good time on each of them. They will give structure and clarity around creating work and life contentment. I suggest that you take no longer than a couple of weeks to complete it. Why not form a group and move through the visioning and this section with friends? They will also help you remember achievements and passions that you may have forgotten.

Questions

1. With all the insights from this program, how will you include creativity in your personal and professional life?

2. How will you use music to help you achieve this change?

3. What creative insights from this program are you going to include every day to assist you in change?

4. Where will you be in a year's time personally and professionally?

5. How are you going to achieve this?
   (Break down your goals into monthly time frames, e.g. one months time, two months time and so on until you reach 12 months from the date you begin working towards the goal.

6. Break down each month's goals into weekly achievements, e.g. what will you do in week one, week two and so on. This keeps you accountable.

7. What are your passions, personal and professional?

8. What are your professional strengths? Imagine you're educating your clients on your area of expertise.

9. What areas of your professional life do you want to discard?

10. What has stopped you from moving ahead and how can you change this mindset to become more successful?

11. What are the strengths and values in your personal life?

12. What professional development are you going to do to support yourself towards these goals?

13. Is there an area of your personal and professional life that you still haven't opened up to creative success?

14. How could you reach your potential through using the teachings from this program?

15. List all the new ideas that have come up from this program.

16. Which of these ideas will you use immediately to start your creative success program?

17. Which ideas will you use at a later stage?

18. How can you keep these ideas alive and use them another time?

19. Where do you want to be in five years' time, personally and professionally?

20. Where do you want to be in two years' time, personally and professionally?

21. What do you need to earn over the next year to support you in this creative success program?

22. List all the businesses and people you need to network with to accelerate this change. Make a wish list, and even if you think some people may be difficult to approach, put their names down. Once you have put this intention on paper, change can happen.

23. How are you going to approach them? For example, will you join business networking groups, get referrals from past clients, or re-evaluate your marketing?

24. Do you need to look outside the area you live in to make this change happen?

25. How will you research the suitability of new markets for your business?
26. Can you partner or joint venture with a group to take your product or business further?

> *'All our dreams can come true when we have the courage to pursue them.'*
>
> WALT DISNEY

Finale

As you've now moved into the staging of the new re-energised 'You', take a moment to check through your body and ask yourself, *'How do I feel?'* There will be many different learnings from this book and I hope that the most challenging area, Work–Life Balance is beginning to happen for you.

We can all get caught up in living our life the best that we can – and then roadblocks happen for no reason. We can go either way: stumble on exhausted, living and working without changing anything or we can look at our life deeply and make a decision to change the parts that aren't working.

Think about it in terms of 'You – The Production' – a metaphor I refer to throughout this book. You picked up this book because something wasn't working in your life. You then moved along on a journey of creative transformation through The Work–Life Balance Wheel and visioning collage sections of the book. How do you feel, now that your production is about to be staged? Where is your show appearing – a city theatre with luxurious decor and a grand audience? Or out of town in a quirky little space, full of locals looking to be entertained and inspired? Maybe you're going to travel around, showing your production in a variety of theatres and you will adapt it for a variety of stages and audiences.

Show adaptation happens all the time in the performing arts world. When stage shows tour after having played in a theatre for many months, the production must be adapted for sporting arenas and smaller theatres. This need for adaption has been factored into planning the show from day one. It's the same for you. If you have to adapt your work or personal time for different parts of your life, how will you do it?

Planning is critical once your creative vision is complete. When I was in *Jesus Christ Superstar*, we took the show around all the major cities of Australia. It was called a 'concert version' of the show and didn't have all the sets, lighting and costumes. Sometimes the performances were in sporting stadiums, and the show would be on centre court. There would be the smell of sweat in the dressing rooms. The buildings were rather bare and devoid of any theatrical glamour however, as soon as we played the first note, the lights went down and the actors appeared and the magic of the show was present.

When the show shifted into longer running seasons in a theatre in Sydney there was all the glamour and trappings that come with high-end musical shows: a giant stage, enormous back stage area, the smell that theatres have and the bars, which were important for keeping everyone involved, connected. (I went to a 40-year reunion of the original *Jesus Christ Superstar* show in Sydney in 2012. It was a great reminder of where I started many years ago. I had forgotten that at 21 I was a talented flautist in one of the world's greatest shows. It reminded me once again the importance of never forgetting where we come from and our past achievements.)

I suggest at this stage of the book that you go back over The Work–Life Balance Wheel. I imagine that already there are some areas of your life and career that have moved into a more balanced place. So how does it feel to have this validation of more balance in your life?

Some key points to remember

- Always think outside the square to take advantage of every opportunity that comes your way.
- Make every part of your life creative.
- Make a commitment every day to continue creative thinking.
- When problems arise, combine your thinking with creative resources to solve them.
- Follow your passions today. Don't look back in 10 years and say, *'Why didn't I do that?'*
- Keep remembering your achievements.
- Remember to laugh and let out that sassy woman.
- Always have music around.

Here is a quote from a woman I admired, Diana Vreeland, who was a noted columnist and editor in the field of fashion:

'You know the greatest thing is passion, without it what have you got? I mean if you love someone you can love them as much as you can love them. But if it isn't passion it isn't burning, it isn't on fire, you haven't lived.'

There has never been a better time for women to truly acknowledge their inner power in all aspects of personal and professional life. As you've read, our inner power and passion is the essence that drives transformation and can work in conjunction with professional skills and training. This book has shown you how important it is to not underestimate our desires to live a life that fulfils; to trust and stand strong when we decide to embrace the intersection between business and creativity. Live, love and grow the creative inspirational woman in you.

I look forward to hearing your stories of transformation. Please feel free to email me at sally@ccdirections.com.au.

To do list

About you

Work-Life Balance Score

Action plan from Visioning Program

Creative inspirations/insights

About the Author

Sally began her professional life as a flautist before hearing problems stopped a promising career. She was headhunted by a Melbourne department store to reinvigorate their homewares department after having launched and run her own successful gourmet cookware shop.

Combining this business experience with her passion for the performing arts, she then sought and won the coveted role of Head of Business Development for The Australian Ballet. Here she became aware of the intersection between business and creative thinking to help unlock the mind and bring forward creative solutions to business challenges.

After leaving the ballet and studying psychotherapy, Sally set up *Creating Encores*. She specialises in helping businesses and individuals use high-performance techniques to produce personal and business problem-solving solutions.

Sally has a proven methodology and a wealth of experience in guiding women out of a tangle of doubt and fear towards self-belief and professional and personal life purpose.

Sally is available for:

- Business coaching
  - › Strategy sessions
  - › 3, 6, 12 months one-on-one coaching and on Skype
- Full and half day programs
  - › Corporate Team Work–Life Balance programs
  - › Corporate Team Visioning programs
  - › Facilitation of groups
- Speaking engagements
- Partnerships and joint ventures

Website: www.creatingencores.co
LinkedIn: SallyArnold
Facebook: creatingencores
Skype: sallyaarnold

Printed in Australia
AUOC02n0911061114
264109AU00007B/7/P